Aubrey H. Whitehouse Series no. 2

Perspectives on the Qur'an
*A Collection of Essays in honour of
Aubrey H Whitehouse*

Editor

Ruth J Nicholls

Arthur Jeffery Centre for the Study of Islam
Melbourne School of Theology
An affiliated college of the Australian College of Theology

Perspectives on the Qur'an: A Collection of Essays in honour of Aubrey H. Whitehouse

ISBN - 978-0-9876154-9-7

© 2018 Melbourne School of Theology Press. All rights reserved.

Series Editor
Ruth Nicholls

Photograph of Aubrey Whitehouse with thanks to Annette Cook.

Production and Cover Design
Ho-yuin Chan

Publishing Services
Published by MST Press
Thanks to Richard Shumack for his publishing services.

Arthur Jeffery Centre for the Study of Islam
Melbourne School of Theology
5 Burwood Highway, Wantirna, Victoria, 3152, Australia.
PO Box 6257, Vermont South, Victoria, 3133, Australia
Ph: +61 3 9881 7800, Fax: +61 3 9800 0121
info@JefferyCentre.mst.edu.au,

Opinions and conclusions published are those of the authors and do not necessarily represent the views of the Arthur Jeffery Centre for the Study of Islam or its Editors. This publication is purely an information medium, to inform interested parties of religious trends, discussions and debates. The Melbourne School of Theology Press affirms the free expression of the religious convictions of its authors but rejects hatred towards any persons or religious group.

The publications in the A. H. Whitehouse Series of books from the Arthur Jeffery Centre for the Study of Islam and MST Press are:

Do You Remember ...? Recollections Reflections [1]
Aubrey H. Whitehouse

Perspectives on the Qur'an: A Collection of Essays in honour of Aubrey H. Whitehouse
Aubrey H. Whitehouse Series no. 2
Editor: Ruth Nicholls

Topical Concordance to the Qur'an
Aubrey H. Whitehouse Series no. 3
Translation: Aubrey H. Whitehouse (reprint)
Foreword: Ruth Nicholls

---

[1] This is a reflection on the author's experiences in Egypt, from 1935–1956

ARTHUR JEFFERY CENTRE FOR THE STUDY OF ISLAM,
Melbourne School of Theology, Australia

Formerly known as the Centre for the Study of Islam and Other Faiths it was renamed the Arthur Jeffery Centre for the Study of Islam in 2016. Arthur Jeffery. was an Australian Methodist missionary who first went to India and ultimately developed proficient in 19 languages. A contemporary of Samuel Zwemer, Jeffery became a recognized scholar of Islam who was invited to join the staff of the American University in Cairo. His book The Foreign Vocabulary of the Qur'an which was first printed in 1938 still stands as the standard text in the field.

The Arthur Jeffery Centre for the Study of Islam is the only such Centre in Australia. Through its team of expert scholars and teachers of Islam it provides a variety of resources at both academic and public levels for those involved in or desiring to be involved in loving and meaningful engagement with Muslims.

The Centre is responsible for designing, preparing and teaching subjects approved by the Australian College of Theology at undergraduate and postgraduate levels relating to Islam. The Centre also aims for academic excellence through its publications which include not only scholarly works but also for those who desire to increase their understanding of Islam. As part of its public engagement the Centre also holds open seminars and events, often joining with others sharing a similar vision and ethos. Staff are also available to speak at public programs.

In 2018 the Centre celebrates 10 years of operation and has established itself as a major centre for postgraduate studies in Islam.

For further information about the Centre and its activities, as well as opportunities to study Islam in a Christian context at both an undergraduate and postgraduate levels, email info@JefferyCentre.mst.edu.au

TABLE OF CONTENTS

FOREWORD	**IX**
INTRODUCING AUBREY WHITEHOUSE	**XV**
WHAT THE QUR'AN SAYS	
AUBREY WHITEHOUSE	1
REFLECTIONS ON A CHRONOLOGICAL READING OF THE QUR'AN	
PAUL FREEMAN	15
HOW THE QUR'AN CAME TO BE	
DR ANTHONY MCROY	25
THE CHALLENGE OF THE SANA'A MANUSCRIPTS TO THE MUSLIM CLAIM OF THE PERFECT QUR'AN	
CHRISTINA A. CIRUCCI M.D.	41
THE BIBLE, THE QUR'AN, AND THE SPACE IN BETWEEN: TELLING THE STORY	
BRENT NEELY	53
COMMENTARIES ON THE QUR'AN: VIEWS OF BIBLICAL CHARACTERS AND CHRISTIANS	
PETER RIDDELL	63
THE USE AND ABUSE OF THE QUR'AN IN CHRISTIAN MISSION	
MARK ANDERSON	83

FOREWORD

Ruth Nicholls[1]

The impetus for this volume came when the Arthur Jeffery Centre for the Study of Islam was given some of the writings of Aubrey Whitehouse. Whitehouse was a former lecturer in Islam at the college, now the Melbourne School of Theology, from which he graduated in 1935. Following his graduation, he went to Egypt where he immersed himself in the study of Arabic and Islam. Growing out of his experience, he wrote an introductory course to the study of Arabic which included cassettes. While in Egypt, he wrote various pamphlets explaining the Christian position in relation to questions and objections posed by the Muslims with whom he and his fellow workers interacted. Not surprisingly, he also wrote an *Introduction to the Study of Islam* which was produced in a teach-yourself, question-and-answer format. To assist others, he also wrote a small pamphlet entitled *What the Qur'an teaches*.

In reviewing the work, the Arthur Jeffery Centre for the Study of Islam noted that it provides a valuable introduction to the Qur'an from the Christian perspective. In these days when matters relating to Islam are "hot press" it is important to be able to refer to resources which are both reliable and trustworthy. As a scholar of Islam, Whitehouse is both reliable and trustworthy. What he presents in his paper is well-researched and emerges from his own experience and studies of Islam. His presentation can be corroborated from other reliable sources.

Further, any genuine study of Islam must include an understanding of the Qur'an and its teaching especially from the perspective of those for whom it is their holy book and who

---

[1] Dr Ruth Nicholls is the Administrator of and a Research Fellow at the Arthur Jeffery Centre for the Study of Islam, Melbourne School of Theology. Ruth spent many years in Christian service in a Muslim country.

endeavour to live by its precepts. For Christians who want to communicate effectively with their Muslim neighbours, such an understanding is of primary importance. But how or where does one begin? This small volume aims to provide a base from which further study and exploration can occur. While it is not feasible in this volume to provide a detailed study of the Qur'an and its teaching, it is possible to provide an overview, especially as it relates to Christians. Questions relating to the Qur'an must consider its compilation, "inspiration", interpretation and use. So, it is these issues that are addressed, though it should not be assumed that this edition provides the final answers to any of the questions. Indeed, each of the papers raises more questions and invites further exploration.

Briefly, the contents of the volume are selective. Since the volume is in honour of Aubrey Whitehouse, it begins with his essay on "What the Qur'an says". Whitehouse summarises the content of the Qur'an with a broad sweep, aiming to primarily inform Christians of its contents. So, it is not surprising then, that his survey includes Qur'anic teaching about Jesus. What Whitehouse has written is an overview and needs to be supplemented by a more detailed exploration. To understand a Muslim's perspective of the Qur'an, reading the Qur'an itself and understanding how it is exegeted is a further step.

However, while for a Muslim the recitation of the Qur'an is considered beauty *par excellence,* for most trying to read a "translation"—for a Qur'an can only truly be understood in Arabic, so it is claimed—it is a difficult exercise. Some find it easier if the "translated" Qur'an has been ordered in (one of) the chronological sequences[2], though even then it can be a chore. Nevertheless, in essence, anything that will aid the non-Arabic reader in their understanding must be to their advantage. Consequently, this edition includes a paper which reflects on a reading of the Qur'an based on one of those chronologies. Indeed, there are several

---

[2] There are a number of chronological sequences of the chapters (*suras*) that have been proposed for the Qur'an. One of the most accepted is that by Theodor Nöldeke. For a helpful article on the chronology of the Qur'an see Peter G. Riddell, "Reading the Qur'an Chronologically" in *Islamic Studies Today: Essays in Honour of Andrew Rippin,* ed. Majid Daneshgar & Walid A. Saleh, Brill, Leiden, 2017, pp297–316, especially p304.

editions of the Qur'an in English which are ordered according to the translator's understanding of the chronology. Consequently, the ordering of the chapters (*sura*) can vary.[3]

The very issue of the lack of a chronological structure of the Qur'an immediately raises an important question. How did the Qur'an come into being? One of the claims that is made of the Qur'an is that it stands alone in its absolute authenticity[4], that it is eternal and has existed unchanged and uncorrupted since its initial revelation. Also, some would consider that the Qur'an is above such examination or questioning. On the other hand, the compilation of the Qur'an is a complex issue and there is not space within this volume to fully explore this topic. Anthony McRoy approaches the issue as a historian and raises some very pertinent issues. Alongside McRoy's article is another that looks in more detail at the Sana'a manuscripts, which, while written in earlier years of the debate, throws some interesting light on Qur'anic issues.

Given that the Qur'an is considered a holy book, the question that arises is how is it "holy"? Muslims claim that the Prophet received his revelations from Allah, so how is that to be understood? Brent Neely explores that question in his article by asking some very important questions: "*What is divine inspiration and what would it look like in a book anyhow? What about genre issues? What is the structure of faith; the character and purpose of God; the predicament of humanity; the nature of salvation?*" [italic sic] (p54). These questions, as he notes, are different from those that are usually raised such as accuracy/error and miracles of language. The purpose of Neely's article is to examine the "contrasting notions of Salvation History" found in the Bible and Qur'an. For Christians, interacting with Muslims, this provides a valuable insight.

Peter Riddell's article takes us to the heart of understanding the Qur'an from a Muslim's perspective—exegesis of the Qur'anic text. Riddell's article is both a model—what needs to be done and how it is done—as well as being a guide to the type of issues that

---

[3] cf. *The Koran,* translated with notes by N.J. Dawood, 1974, Harmondsworth, Middlesex, Penguin Books; *The Koran,* translated by J. M. Rodwell, 1950, London, Dent & Sons.
[4] Arif Humayun, The Quran – History of Text:
https://www.alislam.org/library/articles/quran-history-of-text/ cited 31 August, 2017.

one might encounter. Again, it is an introduction which invites us to explore further.

The final article in this volume considers a very important question, especially for Christians. Mark Anderson raises the challenge of using the Qur'an and associated materials in a way that is both honouring to Muslims for whom Islam is the religion in which they have found their life and living and at the same time honouring Christ. While his article includes critical evaluation it also provides a basis from which to reach out to Muslims in love and friendship.

Aubrey Whitehouse was a student of Islam who strove to interact meaningfully and sensitively with Muslims as a Christian. The purpose of this collection of essays, in honour of Whitehouse as a former student of and lecturer at the Melbourne School of Theology, is to reflect his heart and passion for Muslims. This small volume aims to assist you on your journey of loving and caring for Muslims while at the same time bringing glory and honour to Christ.

Aubrey H. Whitehouse
18 April 1908 - 26 March 1997

INTRODUCING AUBREY WHITEHOUSE

The Arthur Jeffery Centre for the Study of Islam was originally established in 2007 as the Centre for the Study of Islam and Other Faiths as an integral part of the Melbourne School of Theology (MST). Over the many years of MST's varied history interaction with Islam and the study of Islam has played a role. Since many of the graduates of the School were taking varying roles in Christian ministry in contexts where Islam was present, the need to understand Islam and be equipped to interact with Muslims was recognized through introducing courses on Islam. Consequently, lecturers who themselves had interacted with Islam in some way gave students insights into Islam. With the growing awareness of Islam, the migration of Muslims beyond traditional locations, and the increasing political activity of Muslims, the need to establish an Australian Centre for the Study of Islam for Christians engaging with Islam led to the formation of the Centre for the Study of Islam and Other Faiths. However, over time, the focus on Islam became stronger and the Centre changed its name in 2016 to the Arthur Jeffery Centre for the Study of Islam.

An early student to graduate from the college, Aubrey Whitehouse went to Egypt where he became proficient in Arabic and grew in his understanding of Islam as he shared the message of the Christian gospel among the largely Muslim population. While in Egypt he wrote a number of pamphlets, designed to elucidate issues relating to Muslim objections to the Christian gospel. After leaving Egypt, Whitehouse became the Principal of the Lebanon Bible Institute where he continued to deepen his understanding of Islam as he related to Muslims.

After his return (with his wife) to Australia, he wrote an *Introduction to Islam*. He also published a course on Arabic (cassettes included) which had had its embryonic beginning in Egypt. In addition, he was invited by Neville Anderson, the then Principal of BCV (now MST), who himself had worked among Muslims, to lecture on Islam at the School. In that capacity, Whitehouse prepared an extensive and annotated bibliography which, while dated, remains an invaluable resource which is currently housed in the School's library. As a lecturer in Islam he is one of the forerunners of the current Centre. Whitehouse's legacy includes a number of articles on Islam of which "What the Qur'an says" is one. Whitehouse also translated *A Topical Concordance to the Qur'an* which the Arthur Jeffery Centre is planning to republish.

An added dimension to Whitehouse's story is that he himself was a student of Arthur Jeffery, after whom the Centre is named.

Thus, one of the purposes of this work is to honour and recognise one who gave himself to study Islam and was keen to share with others what he had learnt. In addition, it acknowledges his status as a past student, a lecturer of Islam and a forerunner of the Arthur Jeffery Centre for the Study of Islam, Melbourne School of Theology.

Ruth Nicholls
Administrator
Arthur Jeffery Centre for the Study of Islam

WHAT THE QUR'AN SAYS[1]

Aubrey Whitehouse[2]

THE QUR'AN, the sacred book of the Muslims, is believed to have been revealed to Muhammad by the angel Gabriel "piecemeal" as the occasion required. It was received and passed on orally, and was not committed to writing until after the death of Muhammad. The word "Qur'an" is derived from the Arabic word *qura* which means "to read" or "to recite," and its use in connection with the Muslim scriptures is based on the first word of *Sura* 96, "Read, in the name of thy Lord!"[3] The first five verses of this *sura*, although placed towards the end of the Qur'an, are generally regarded as the beginning of the revelation.

The Qur'an says ... ...

FOR THE MUSLIM, the Qur'an is the Word of God in the most literal sense. Muhammad was merely the recipient of that word and passed it on. It bears no imprint of the prophet's character at all, and nothing could be more blasphemous to the Muslim than

---

[1] The Arthur Jeffery Centre for the Study of Islam and the Melbourne School of Theology Press are aware that this document, which was originally written by Aubrey H. Whitehouse and of which they hold a copy, has been reproduced in another publication without acknowledging the original source or its author. A. H. Whitehouse was both a student and a lecturer at what is now known as the Melbourne School of Theology. The Arthur Jeffery Centre for the Study of Islam has contacted the original publishers of the work who alerted them to the unacknowledged reproduction of the work.

[2] Aubrey Whitehouse spent many years working in several Islamic contexts. He became proficient in Arabic and was a student of Islam.

[3] All quotations are taken from the translation into English by E. H. Palmer, *The Koran* -The World's Classics, No. 328, Oxford University Press. The Palmer translation of the Qur'an is available on the internet.
http://www.sacred-texts.com/isl/sbe06/index.htm cited 14 August, 2017
Ed: It should be noted that the numbering of verses in English translations of the Qur'an can vary significantly, sometimes within a range of at least five verses.

to attribute the Qur'an, even in a secondary sense, to Muhammad, as, for example, the writings of the Bible are attributed to their human authors.

In seeking to understand what the Qur'an says in matters of religious belief and practice, it is essential that we recognise that the Qur'an is not the only source of authority for the Muslim. The traditions of Muhammad's sayings and conduct are also authoritative. Nevertheless, the Qur'an is the primary source. Although it does not deal with all aspects of life for which Islam legislates, in those areas in which it speaks, it speaks with absolute divine authority. It should be noted however, that in the classical theory, it is possible for a text in the Qur'an to be abrogated by a "genuine" prophetic tradition of a later date.

The Testimony of the Qur'an to Itself

It would be well to start this study with a reference to something of what is recorded in the Qur'an about the book itself. It will be noted from these selections, representative of many other verses in the Qur'an, that it is repeatedly asserted that the Qur'an is a revelation direct from God. The following verses were "revealed" to Muhammad in reply to objections that it was he who had produced it.

> *Say. 'If mankind and Jinns united together to bring the like of this Qur'an they could not bring the like though they should back each other up.' (Q17:90)*

> *This Qur'an could not have been devised by any beside God; but it verifies what was before it ... do they say 'he (i.e. Muhammad) hath devised it?' Say then 'bring a surah (chapter) like it—— and call, if ye can, on other than God, if ye do tell the truth'. Q10:39*

The reference to the fact of the Qur'an verifying what came before it, is another oft-repeated claim for the Qur'an that it confirms and carries on the revelation previously "sent down" in the *Torah* (Old Testament in general) and in the *Injil* (New Testament). Typical of these is the following verse:

> *He (God) has sent down to thee the Book in truth, confirming what was before it, and has revealed the Law (Torah) and the Gospel (Injil) before for the guidance of men. Q3:2*

In reply to the contention of some of Muhammad's opponents that there were obvious contradictions in the Qur'an, a verse was "revealed" to settle the matter, which states concerning these differences—

> *God blots out what He will, or He confirms; and with Him is the Mother of the Book.* Q13:39

The "Mother of the Book" refers to the eternal original kept in heaven, sometimes called the "Preserved Tablet" or the "Laid-up Book" as in Q56:79.

This is the famous verse of abrogation. In general, it means that in the case of "contradiction," the later verse replaces the earlier verse, the argument being that the earlier verse was appropriate to the early stages of Muhammad's mission, but needed modifying later on. The verse on religious freedom mentioned at the end of this study is an example of this. The difficulty, of course, lies in determining which was in fact the earlier verse.

> *Verily this is the honourable Qur'an in the Laid-up Book. Let none touch it but the purified! A revelation from the Lord of the Worlds.* Q56:77-80

One further claim of the Qur'an for itself should be noticed: namely, that it was revealed in Arabic, the language of the people to whom it was sent down, and not in a "foreign" language, as were the *Torah* and *Injil* of the Jews and the Christians.

> *A.L.R[4]. These are the signs of the perspicuous book. Verily we have revealed it, an Arabic Qur'an, haply ye may understand.* Q12:2

The Testimony of the Qur'an to Previous Holy Books

Islam teaches that in all there were 104 holy books "sent down" on prophets of old, but of these only four are extant: the *Torah* (the Law or Old Testament in general), the *Zabour* (the Psalms), the *Injil* (the Gospel or the New Testament in general), and

---

[4]Ed. A.L.R that is Alif, Lam, and Ra' are the names of the Arabic letters which are found at the beginning of some of the *suras* of the Qur'an. They are considered "mystic symbols, about whose meaning there is no authoritative explanation." (p477, *The Meaning of the Holy Qur'an*, Abdullah Yusuf 'Ali, new edition with Revised Translation and Commentary, AH 1409/1989 AC, Maryland, Amana Publications.

the Qur'an. There are over 120 references in the Qur'an to the scriptures of the Jews and the Christians, testifying to their being genuine revelations from God. The Jews and Christians were generally known as "the people of the Book."

It is important that those who have dealings with Muslims should know that Muhammad did not claim to bring a completely new revelation, or to establish a new religion. His concern was to bring his people back to the original religion professed and preached by all the prophets from Adam onwards. This religion was Islam, and those who professed it were Muslims (Arabic: *Muslimun*). The Arabic word simply meant to resign or commit oneself (to God), and did not at first refer to Muhammad's followers. The following verse is an illustration of this attitude:

> *Say ye "we believe in God, and what has been revealed to Abraham, and Ishmael, and Isaac, and Jacob, and the Tribes, and what was brought to Moses, and Jesus, and what was brought unto the prophets from their Lord; we will not distinguish between any one of them, and unto Him are we resigned* (Arabic: *Muslimun*)". Q2:130

Typical of verses which indicate the acceptance by Muhammad of the existing holy books is that found in Q4:162.

> *Verily we have inspired thee as we inspired Noah and the prophets after him, and as we inspired Abraham, and Ishmael, and Jacob, and the Tribes, and Jesus, and Job, and Jonas, and Aaron, and Solomon; and to David did we give the Psalms.*

His dependence on the existing holy books is even more clearly indicated in Q10:94:

> *And if thou art in doubt of that which we have sent down unto thee, ask those who read the book before thee* (i.e. Jews and Christians).

The Christian is, therefore, in a very strong position in inviting the Muslim to read the Scriptures, for the Qur'an clearly testifies to their authenticity, and, as we have seen, even advises the perplexed Muslim to consult the Christians about matters of religion which he does not understand. At this point, however, we meet the first barrier between the Muslim and the Christian. For, if the Muslim were, in fact, to consult the Christian or to read the Christian's book, he would find obvious contradictions to the teaching of the Qur'an. This is a serious problem to the Muslim for, if the Qur'an and the other "books"— the *Torah*, *Zabour* and the

Injil— are all from God, and if the Qur'an is a confirmation of the message of those books, then there should be harmony and continuity, and not contradiction. The only honest conclusion which can be arrived at from the existence of contradictions is that either the previous scriptures, or the Qur'an, are not, in fact, revelations from God. But that is quite contrary to the plain teaching of the Qur'an. To escape from this dilemma, the Muslims have introduced the theory of the corruption of the existing copies of the scriptures of the Jews and Christians. On this theory, the references in the Qur'an to the previous scriptures are to the original books, and not to the present "corrupt" copies. In support of this theory the following verse from the Qur'an is sometimes quoted:

> *And verily amongst them is a sect who twist their tongues concerning the book, (i.e. pervert it) that ye may reckon it to be from the book. They say "it is from God" but it is not from God.* Q3:73

One illustration of how this alleged corruption occurred is the Muslim contention that the reference in John 16:7, and other places, to the Holy Spirit as the Comforter, was originally a prophecy concerning the coming of Muhammad, another form of whose name is Ahmad. The verse in the Qur'an which Muslims commonly refer to in this context reads:

> *And when Jesus the son of Mary said, "O Children of Israel! Verily, I am the Apostle of God to you, verifying the Law that was before me and giving you glad tidings of an apostle who shall come after me, whose name shall be Ahmad."* Q61:6

The Muslim contention is that the Greek word *Paracletos* translated "Comforter" in the *Injil*, is a corruption of the original word *Periclutos*, the meaning of which in Arabic is stated to be "Ahmad".

This, and all other alleged corruptions of the scriptures, can easily be shown to be without foundation, from the simple fact that complete manuscripts of the Greek New Testament, which go back two centuries or more before the time of Muhammad, are in existence today. These substantiate the text of our present-day (Arabic) versions, and not the Qur'anic variant.

The Affirmations of the Qur'an

In some respects, the affirmations of the Qur'an are as important as its denials, though less well known. These positive statements fix the picture of Christ and Christian teaching firmly in the Muslim mind. The following are some of the most important affirmations of the Qur'an:

1. **The Fall**

   And we said 'O Adam dwell thou and thy wife in Paradise and eat therefrom amply as you wish; but do not draw near this tree or ye will be of the transgressors'. And Satan made them backslide therefrom and drove them out from what they were in, and we said "Go down one of you the enemy of the other ...' Q2:34. (See also 7:15ff and 20:113-119)

   In this connection, we should note, in passing, that the Qur'an knows nothing of any earthly paradise in Eden. Paradise is in Heaven, and it was from Heaven to earth that Adam and Eve literally fell.

2. **The Virgin Birth of Christ**

   Some of the longest chapters in the Qur'an are concerned with Jesus and Mary and the annunciation of the birth of Christ. Among them are the "chapter of Women", and the "chapter of Mary", and the "chapter of Imran's family". The following are some extracts from these last two chapters-

   When the angel said, "O Mary! Verily God gives thee the glad tidings of a word from Him; his name shall be the Messiah, Jesus the son of Mary ...". She said, "Lord! how can I have a son when man has not yet touched me?" He said, "Thus God creates what He pleaseth. When He decrees a matter He only says "BE", and it is ..." Q3:40–48 and 19:19-21.

   And mention in the Book, Mary ... we sent unto her our spirit; and he took the semblance of a well-made man ... said he, "I am only a messenger of thy Lord to bestow on thee a pure boy." Said she, "How can I have a boy when no man hath touched me and when I am no harlot?" He said, "Thus saith thy Lord, it is easy for me ..." So she conceived him and retired with him into a remote place ... Q19:16–21 and 66:12.

3. **The assertion that Christ is a created being**

> *Verily, the likeness of Jesus with God is as the likeness of Adam. He created him from earth, then He said to him, BE, and he was ...* Q3:52

Although the obvious intention of this verse is to establish the fact of Christ's being merely a man, there could be some ambiguity as to whether the phrase "He created him" refers to Adam or Jesus. If the reference is to Adam, there is, of course, no contradiction of the Christian scriptures here. Muslims, however, generally regard this as referring to Jesus. In any case, this is a verse to which the Christian's best reply is to state that the Christian scriptures also compare Christ with Adam, not because He is a created being like Adam, but that, like Adam, He is the head of a new creation.

4   The miracles of Christ

There is a good deal in the Qur'an (and still more in other Muslim writings) of the miracles performed by Christ by way of authenticating His mission. But they are always stated to be "by the permission of God." There is no recognition of the fact that Christ had any inherent divine power. The following verse is a sample of these statements:

> *O Jesus, Son of Mary! Remember my favours towards thee and towards thy mother when I aided thee with the Holy Ghost, till thou didst speak to men in the cradle and when grown up ... when thou didst create of clay, as it were, the likeness of a bird, by my power, and didst blow thereon, and it became a bird, and when thou didst heal the blind from birth, and the leprous, by my permission; and when thou didst bring forth the dead by my permission.* Q5:109–110

The Denials of the Qur'an

The denials of the Qur'an relate to the basic doctrines concerning Christ. We can only appreciate how serious and important these are when we remember that, to a Muslim, they are not merely the teachings of his religion, but they express the word of God in God's own words.

1.   Denial of the Trinity, and of the Deity of Christ

The Messiah, Jesus the Son of Mary, is but the apostle of God, and His Word which He cast into Mary, and a spirit from Him! Believe then in God and His apostles, and say not "Three." Have done! It

> *were better for you. God is only one God, celebrated be His praises, that He should beget a son ...* Q4:169 and Q6:101–2:106

> *And when God said, "O Jesus, Son of Mary! Is it thou who didst say to men 'take me and my mother for two gods beside God?'" He said, "I celebrate Thy praise! What ails me that I should say what I have no right to?"* Q5:116

It is well to note here, that what the Muslim rejects as the false teaching of some Christian sects, the Christian also rejects; for what Muhammad rejects here is not the teaching of Christianity, but what he thought was its teaching. He understood the Christians referred to in the above verse to believe that the Trinity consisted of Father, Mother (Mary) and Son. The extreme veneration accorded to Mary by the Christians Muhammad met, no doubt gave rise to this view. The phrase "I celebrate Thy praise" is a strong form of oath.

2. Denial of the Sonship of Christ

There are many Qur'anic verses which stress the absolute unity of God, and by implication deny the sonship of Christ, and there are others, such as the Chapter of Unity, which follows, which deny the possibility of sonship in general.

> *Say, He is God alone! God the Eternal! He begets not and is not begotten! Nor is there like unto Him anyone.* Q112

There are also a number of verses where the sonship of Christ is specifically denied, such as the verse quoted above in connection with the Trinity, and the following verse:

> *That is, Jesus the Son of Mary –by the word of truth whereon ye do dispute! God could not take to Himself any son!* Q19:5

The seriousness of the Muslim view of the Christian doctrines of the Trinity, and of the deity of Christ, is seen in the following verse:

> *Verily, God pardons not associating aught with Him, but He pardons anything short of that to whomsoever He pleases! but he who associates aught with God, he hath devised a mighty sin.* Q4:51

Although the sin of "shirk" associating anyone with God as a co-deity is the most deadly of all sins, what makes the Christian doctrine more blasphemous in the eyes of the Muslim, is the description of Christ as the Son of God. This arises from the fact that the Muslim—or more properly Muhammad—could only think of sonship in terms of the human relationship of father and mother. It is probably true to say that the Muslim is less offended by our ascribing Deity to Christ, than by our designation of Him as the Son of God.

3. Denial of the crucifixion of Christ

This is probably the best-known and most basic of all Muslim denials, not least because it is so categorical.

> *And for their misbelief and for their saying about Mary a mighty calumny, and for their saying "verily we have killed the Messiah, Jesus the Son of Mary, the apostle of God ...", but they did not kill him, and they did not crucify him, but a similitude was made for them ... they did not kill him, for sure! Nay, God raised him to Himself! for God is mighty and wise.* Q4:155ff.

No Muslim can side-step the categorical denial of the death of Christ contained in this passage, in spite of the fact that it poses two main difficulties for the modern educated Muslim. The first is the basic assertion that Christ did not die, an assertion which many are prepared to deny, or to ascribe to a misinterpretation. Arising out of this dilemma is the equally difficult position that, if Christ did not die, He obviously would be far superior to prophets, such as Muhammad, who did die. To escape from such a conclusion, Muslim traditions speak of the future return of Christ to this world, His embracing of Islam, and His subsequent death. This position is based on an interpretation of such a verse as the following

> *Peace upon me the day I was born, and the day I die, and the day I shall be raised up alive. That is, Jesus the Son of Mary.* Q19:34–35

To make this verse fit in with this theory, the most natural thing would be to alter the order of the words, so that the phrase "the day I die" follows the phrase "the day I shall be raised up alive," but such an alteration would be a sin to the Muslim as it involves an alteration to the "revealed" word of God. In any case, it is a weak argument, as the same words are used in the same chapter, a few verses previously, in connection with John the son of Zachariah (John the Baptist), and no-one would think of altering the order of the words in this case (see Q19:15).

The Teaching of the Qur'an

Most of the quotations above have a direct relationship to the teaching of the Jewish and Christian scriptures. There is also, in the Qur'an, a mass of teaching about subjects which are the concern of the Bible, but which are dealt with in the Qur'an independently or ostensibly so. The following are some of the subjects which the Qur'an speaks about.

1. **The Devil**

   His origin and works are described in Q7:10 ff.

   And we created you, then we fashioned you, then we said to the angels, "Adore Adam," and they adored, save Iblis (the devil), who was not one of those who did adore. Said He, "What hinders thee from adoring when I order thee?" He said "I am better than he; thou hast created me from fire. and him thou hast created out of clay." Said He, "Then go down therefrom (i.e. from heaven). What ails thee that thou shouldest be big with pride?" Said he, "For that thou hast led me unto now, I will lay in wait for them (mankind) in Thy straight path!" He (God) said, "Go forth therefrom, despised, expelled; whoso follows thee, I will surely fill hell with you altogether."

2. **Hell**

   I will boil him in hell fire! and what shall make thee know what is hell fire? It will not leave and will not let alone. It scorches the flesh, over it are nineteen (angels). Q74:25–30

   Those who misbelieve, into hell they shall be gathered! that God may distinguish the vile from the good, and may put the vile, some on top of the other, and heap up all together, and put it into hell! These are those who lose! Q8:3ff and Q74:44–48

   Faces on that day ... shall boil with a burning fire! They shall be given to drink from a boiling spring! No food shall they have save the foul thorn, which shall not fatten nor avail against hunger! Q88:4–8

3. **Heaven (Paradise)**

   Faces on that day shall be comfortable, contented with their past endeavours—in a lofty garden wherein they shall hear no foolish word; wherein is a flowing fountain; wherein are couches raised on high. And goblets set down, and cushions arranged, and carpets spread. Q88:9–15

The fellows on the right hand—what lucky fellows! ... These are they who are brought nigh, in gardens of pleasure! ... and gold weft couches, reclining on them face to face, around them shall go eternal youths, with goblets and ewers and a cup of flowing wine! No headache shall they fear therefrom, nor shall their wits be dimmed! and fruits such as they deem best! and flesh of fowl such as they desire! and bright and large-eyed maids like hidden pearls! a reward for what they have done. They shall hear no folly there and no sin ... verily we have produced them (the celestial damsels) a production, and made them virgins, darlings of equal age (with their spouses) for the fellows of the right! Q56:7–39

4. Resurrection and Judgement

We will place just balances upon the resurrection day, and no soul shall be wronged at all, even though it be the weight of a grain of mustard seed, we will bring it, for we are good at reckoning up. Q21:48

Eschatology forms a very large part of the teaching of the Qur'an, especially in the early chapters which reflect Muhammad's early preaching at Mecca. There are lengthy accounts of the resurrection in chapters Q75; 81:1–19; 82; 83:4–20; 84:1–19. The following is an extract from Q81:

And when the stars do fall, and when the mountains are moved ... and when the beasts shall be crowded together, and when the seas shall surge up, and when the souls shall be paired with bodies, and when the child that was buried alive shall be asked for what sin she was slain, and when the pages shall be spread out, and when the heavens shall be flayed, and when hell shall be set ablaze, and when paradise shall be brought nigh, the soul shall know what it has produced! Q81:2, 5–14

4. Forgiveness

There is very little in the Qur'an about forgiveness in comparison with other subjects which are dealt with at length. From what is mentioned it is clear that it is regarded as a quite arbitrary act of God which has little, if any, moral basis, and requires no act of redemption or reconciliation. The following are some of the few verses dealing with this subject:

Verily, God pardons not associating aught with Him, but He pardons anything short of that to whomsoever He pleases, but he who associates aught with God, he hath devised a mighty sin. Q4:51 and 116

> For those who believe and do right, for them is forgiveness and a great hire. Q35:8

5. Predestination (Fate)

This is very closely linked with the teaching on forgiveness. This appears in such verses as the following:

> Verily God leads astray whom He pleases and guides whom He pleases ... Q35:9

> Whom He pleases does God lead astray, and whom He pleases He places on the right way. Q6:39

> God leads whom He will astray and guards whom He will, and He is the Mighty, the Wise. Q14:4

The same sentiments are expressed in Q74:34.

6. Prayer

The Muslim prays five times a day. This is believed to be in accordance with the instructions of the Qur'an, but in no one verse in the Qur'an are all the five times mentioned together. Prayer, for the Muslim, is much more of a religious exercise than prayer as the Christian knows it. It must be said in Arabic, and the same forms and words are used every time. The following are some of the Qur'anic verses referring to prayer

> O ye who believe! When ye rise up to prayer wash your faces, and your hands as far as the elbows, and wipe your heads, and your feet down to the ankles ... But if ye ... cannot find water, then take fine surface sand and wipe your faces and your hands therewith. Q5:8ff.

The above verses refer to the ceremonial ablutions which must precede prayer, and which Muhammad described as the half of faith and the key to prayer.

> And be thou steadfast in prayer at the two ends of the day, and the (former and latter) parts of the night. Verily good works remove evil works. Q11:116

> But when ye have fulfilled your prayer, remember God, standing and sitting, and lying on your sides; and when ye are in safety, then be steadfast in prayer, prayer is for the believers prescribed and timed. Q4:104

7. Freedom of worship

Although practice may differ a great deal from what is believed, the Qur'an in at least one verse, frequently quoted by Muslims, clearly teaches of freedom of religion, even if only negatively.

> *There is no compulsion in religion; the right way has been distinguished from the wrong.* Q2:258ff

In view of the fact that elsewhere Muslims are exhorted to kill the idolaters wherever they may find them (Q9:5) and, "to fight those who believe not on God ... who do not practice the religion of truth from amongst those to whom the book has been brought" (Q9:29) the verse of abrogation is sometimes brought in to justify this contradiction in attitude. The *Ulama*, or traditional teachers, may still adhere to the doctrine of Jihad, or "holy war," based on these latter verses, but in general, the modern western-educated Muslim would be inclined to regard the first mentioned verse (Q2:258) as representing the true spirit of Islam.

8. Islam is the only religion
Whosoever craves other than Islam for a religion, it surely shall not be accepted from him, and he shall, in the next world, be of those who lose. Q3:17, 79, cf. Q4:115

The foregoing are some of the principal and most widely-known verses of the Qur'an which deal with matters where there is contact or conflict (or both) with the Christian scriptures. There is, of course, much else in the Qur'an that deals with matters of legislation for the Muslim community, as well as stories of the prophets.

There is little order or design in the Qur'an as judged by Western ideas, and although the chanting of the Qur'an in Arabic has a pleasing—even hypnotic—effect on the Arabic-speaking person, this cannot be conveyed in an English translation. Consequently, the average English-reader might well find himself agreeing with Carlyle, that only a sense of duty would carry an Englishman through the Qur'an. Nevertheless, if we really want to understand something of the way the Muslim is conditioned to think of religion, it is a duty to attain to some knowledge of the Qur'an, so that he may be reached with the message of the Gospel.

For Further Reading

Arberry, A. J., 1955, *The Holy Koran,* George Allen & Unwin.

Bell, Richard, 1953, revised by W. M. Watt, 1969, *Introduction to the Qur'an,* Edinburgh University Press.

Bevan Jones, L., 1932, revised 1959, *The People of the Mosque-* Baptist Mission Press, Calcutta.

Dawood, N. J., 1956, *The Koran-Translation,* Penguin Classics.

Palmer, E.H., 1950, *The Koran,* (Translated), The World's Classics, no 328, Oxford University Press.

Parrinder, G., 1965, *Jesus in the Qur'an,* Faber & Faber.

Rodwell, J.M., 1861, *The Koran-Translation,* Everyman's Library (380).

Stanton, W. 1919-reprinted 1969, *The Teaching of the Qur'an,* S.P.C.K..

Watt, W. Montgomery, 1967, *Companion to the Qur'an,* George Allen & Unwin.

REFLECTIONS ON A CHRONOLOGICAL READING OF THE QUR'AN[1]

Paul Freeman[2]

Editor: Because the chapters (*sura*) of the Qur'an are not ordered chronologically in most editions, a reader who reads from beginning to end will miss out on the sequence of Muhammad's life which is reportedly contained in the Qur'an. In order to grasp that sequence, readers need first to read the Meccan chapters, in the order of their compiling, and then read the Medinan chapters which reflect the last ten years of Muhammad's life. One generally accepted chronology was proposed by Theodor Nöldeke. Paul Freeman provides a series of reflections on an initial reading of the Qur'an according to this well-regarded chronology. (The appropriate chapters are listed at the beginning of each section.) In reading the Qur'an it should be noted that God/Allah uses the personal pronouns such as "I, me, we, us."

Reflections on the *Suras* from the First Meccan Period

96, 74, 111, 106, 108, 104, 107, 102, 105, 92, 90, 94, 93, 97, 86, 91, 80, 68, 87, 95, 103, 85, 73, 101, 99, 82, 81, 53, 84, 100, 79, 77, 78, 88, 89, 75, 83, 69, 51, 52, 56, 70, 55, 112, 109, 113, 114, 1

In reading through the Qur'an for the first time in my life, I had many expectations. Firstly, that I would be able to have some context for passages which completely baffle me, such as Q3:44:

---

[1] This article first appeared in the *Centre for the Study of Islam and Other Faiths Bulletin 2015/16* issue no. 8/9, November 2016, pp32–41.
[2] Paul Freeman is a pseudonym. Paul works with a Muslim majority people group in Africa. He is married, has three children and is currently pursuing his Masters in Muslim Studies.

> ...[y]ou were not present among them when they cast lots to see which of them should take charge of Mary, you were not present with them when they argued [about her][3].

I wonder if verses such as these are akin to 1 Pet 3:19, when Jesus "preached to the spirits who were in prison," which is an odd detail that no one knows for certain what is meant. Are there many deep details like this, or is this a characteristic of the mystery in the revelations that Muhammad is relaying? Secondly, I hoped to see how particularly special this book is, and how it presents the Supreme Being.

In reading the first Meccan *suras*, one of my first surprising observations was the frequent reference to judgment. God is almost presented as a Being who eagerly desires to throw sinful beings into hell, anticipating their recompense for their bad behaviour.

> *He has been stubbornly hostile to Our revelation: I will inflict a mounting torment on him ... I will throw him into the scorching Fire* (Q74:16–17, 26)

On this topic, I was surprised at how often in his first Meccan period *suras* on final judgment and the flames or torment of hell are mentioned.

My first response is to postulate that Muhammad's strategy to get people to follow his teaching was a scare tactic. My second thought was that the lack of development in teaching something other than judgment and hell shows that he was not as interested in developing a new religion as may have seemed. Rather, he was wanting his people to move out of their backward polytheistic practices and join with the philosophy of those he looked up to, perhaps, the "People of the Book" and the Jews.

I also noticed that *Suras* 99, 82 and 84 are strikingly similar: they begin describing an earthquake of some sort. The earth is then personified and brings forth its dead who are then judged. Other *suras* include part of this imagery, such as *Sura* 100, which also mentions, "the contents of the earth are thrown out" (v.9) and

---

[3] M.A.S. Abdel Haleem, *The Qur'an, A New Translation,* 2004,2005, Oxford University Press cited on-line at http://www.kaskas.com/home/wp-content/uploads/2013/11/Quran-Abdel-Haleem-Translation-1.pdf cited 10 September, 2015.

judged. A number of other *suras* detail changing planetary and earthly developments before the final judgment, such as Q77:1–13; 69:13–18; 70:8–9 and 56:1–6.

During this early Meccan period this final judgment is often repeated and seems to be the crux of his message. Specific details include: a trumpet sounding (Q74:8–9); no one knowing the hour of judgment except God (Q79:42–44); and those deemed evil being thrown into hell, which will not only be for the evildoers (Q82:14) but also for those who are distracted by the world (Q102:1–8) as well as those negligent of good deeds (Q101:8, 107:1–6).

Another recurring theme is the humbleness of the origin of man, that he was made from a small helpless form: a "clinging form" (Q96:2), a "spurting fluid" (Q86:6), a "droplet" (Q80:19), a "drop of spilt-out sperm, which became a clinging form" (Q75:37–38), an "ejected drop of sperm" (Q53:46); and "dried clay, like pottery" (Q55:14).

My last comment relates to the Qur'an as the uncreated, eternal word of God—an attribute that Christians do not ascribe to the Bible. In reading these first Meccan *suras*, I was struck by how human the style and discourse sounded. *Sura* 55, for example, is so poetic and rhythmic. If God is wholly other, and his uncreated eternal word is the Qur'an, how does it fit so well into human culture? We must maintain that the Qur'an itself must reflect to a degree that God is other and separate from us.

Secondly, how is it that an eternal, uncreated written thing can reference something that is created and did have a beginning? In eternity past, for example, how did the word "pregnant camels" in Q81:4 have any meaning before camels even existed? I realize that I must rest this line of critique in the knowledge of the unknowable mystery of God. Just as I cannot truly fathom the Trinity, the omnipresence of God and how He exists outside of time and space, so I must grant my Muslim friend understanding in the difficulty of expressing divine mysteries, like the confusing nature of the uncreated Qur'an. At least, when a Muslim friend argues against the confusing nature of the Trinity, we can point out that there are likewise confounding aspects in his beliefs.

Reflections on the *Suras* from the Second Meccan Period
54, 37, 71, 76, 44, 50, 20, 26, 15, 19, 38, 36, 43, 72, 67, 23, 21, 25, 17, 27, 18

The second Meccan period *suras* bring new elements to the Qur'anic message. The most notable one is reference to biblical characters such as Moses (Q37:114-122; 44:17-33; 20:9-98; 26:10-68; 19:51-53; 43:46-56; 23:45-49; 21:48-50; 25:35-36; 17:101-104); Noah (Q54:9-15; 37:75-82; 71:1-28; 26:105-122; 23:23-30; 21:76-77; 25:37); Abraham (Q37:83-113; 26:69-89; 15:57-60; 19:41-50; 38:45 43:26; 21:51-70); Adam (Q20:115-123; 15:26-50; 17:61); Lot (Q54:33-40; 37:133-138; 26:160-175; 15:61-77; 21:71-75; 27:54-58); Job (38:41-44; 21:83-84); David and Solomon (Q38:17–26, 30–40; 21:78–82; 27:15–44); Mary and Jesus (Q19:16–34; 43:57–60; 23:50; 21:91); Zechariah (Q19:1–15; 21:89–90); Jonah (Q37:139–148; 21:87–88) and Ishmael (Q19:54–55; 21:85). In many of these *suras*, the use of the stories of biblical prophets, whose messages were taunted and ridiculed by the people, is to encourage Muhammad. They show how he, like the earlier prophets, suffered in the same ways (Q21:41; 25:4–6), including opposition by those who thought Muhammad was bewitched (Q17:47). God's message to Muhammad is that he should keep on warning even though he is just a "lone man" (Q54:23) chosen from among his own people (Q38:4) and not an angel (Q25:7).

Another new emphasis in the second Meccan period *suras* is the idea of God's mercy. Frequently, God is referred to as "Lord of Mercy" (Q43:36, 45, 81; 17:110; 23:75; 67:3, 19, 29; 36:5, 16, 52), and that God is "most merciful" (Q23:109, 118; 21:36, 42, 83; 25:59, 70; 27:11). I also noted some examples of how God is merciful (Q17:66ff. and 18:58–59), including that the Qur'an itself is a mercy (Q17:82). On the other hand, we also read about God withholding mercy (Q23:75–77), leading some to stray (Q18:17b) and appointing adversaries for prophets (Q25:31).

Overall, the overwhelming chorus echoing throughout the second Meccan period *suras* seems to be one of warning disbelievers of coming judgment and hell (Q54:6–8; 37:19–39; 71; 76:4; 44:10–16; 50:20–30; 20:15–16, 74, 100–111; 26:90–104; 19:37–39, 97–98; 38:14–17; 36:48–65; 43:65–67; 72:15, 23–28; 67:6–11; 23:63–67, 101–104; 21:29; 25:11–14,26–29; 17:8, 18, 63, 97–99; 27:90; 18:29, 52, 106). So central is this warning to the message of the Qur'an (at least in this section) that almost every chapter alludes to the coming judgment! At first, I found it paradoxical that there is such an emphasis on judgment when there is also a strong emphasis, as previously noted, on God as the Lord of mercy. Perhaps, the solution to understanding this paradox, is in the mercy of the Qur'an itself, since:

> *Never have We destroyed a town without sending down messengers to warn it* (Q26:208).

The Qur'an speaks of itself as a mercy that could have been taken away (Q17:86–87).

One aspect of God's message that I expected to find much more frequently in the Qur'an was general instructions about how a person should live with his neighbour. I was interested to finally find a small section that addresses this in Q17:22–38. The uniqueness of this passage from the message of the majority of the text through this period makes me wonder if this reflects the aloof, other, distant, unconcerned nature of God that I sense is perceived by my Muslim friends. It seems that Muslims are more concerned about devotion and purity in the general community than personal relationship. This can also be seen in how God permits Job to strike his wife to carry out what he had promised on oath when he was relieved of his suffering in Q38:44 (see M.A.S. Abdel Haleem's note on this verse for its context).[4] We can learn from this verse that after making what should be interpreted as a foolish oath by Job, God is more concerned that he fulfils his oath rather than from keeping Job from striking his wife.

My last observation on this section is the remarkable similarity that 20:105–112 has with Isaiah 40:3–5. Besides the numerous references to biblical characters as previously noted, I wonder to what extent Muhammad had access to the Bible. From previous reading, I understand that there was no Arabic Bible in the sixth and seventh centuries, and Muhammad was illiterate, in any case. However, a Christian or Jew could have recited Isaiah 40 as well as stories of the prophets and Jesus to him using a rough translation.

---

[4] M.A.S. Abdel Haleem, *The Qur'an: A New Translation*, Oxford, Oxford University Press, 2004, p292.

Reflections on the *Suras* from the Third Meccan Period
32, 41, 45, 16, 30, 11, 14, 12, 40, 28, 39, 29, 31, 42, 10, 34, 35, 7, 46, 6, 13

The third Meccan period *suras* are significantly distinct from the previous two periods in three ways: a development in the description of the nature of God; further developments in the understanding of the final judgment; and a development in the perception of Muhammad's prophethood.

In the third Meccan period *suras*, the development of understanding the nature of God is achieved by using two adjectives usually appearing as a "pair" which occur at the end of a story or a statement. These two adjectives make a statement about the nature of God. For example:

> *All that rests by night or by day belongs to him. He is the All Hearing, the All Knowing* (Q6:13)

and

> *No one will receive any help except for those to whom God shows mercy: He is the Mighty, the Merciful Lord.* (Q46:42)

Not every attribute of God mentioned in this way necessarily relates to the subject of the preceding ideas, for example:

> *He has subjected the sun and moon to run their courses for an appointed time; He is truly the Mighty, the Forgiving* (Q39:5).

Other descriptive comments about God that I noted in reading the *suras* of this period include the following:

- the God of the "People of the Book," the Christians, is the same as the God of the Qur'an (Q29:46);
- God is "appreciative" (a strange characteristic to attribute to an all-powerful God) of those who do good (Q42:23);
- God's kingship is associated with this world (Q13:2); and
- God invites everyone to heaven (Q10:25), which contrasts with Satan, who invites everyone to hell (Q35:6).

The final judgment continues to be a dominant theme in Muhammad's message as recorded in the Qur'an. In these third Meccan *suras*, the following statements stood out:

- it is possible to be so sinful that one is unredeemable (Q10:88–89, 90–91);
- heaven may not be eternal (Q11:108; 46:3);
- there will be arguing in hell (Q40:46–50);
- animals will be judged (Q6:38);
- the bad deeds of the righteous will be overlooked (Q46:16); and there is (at least a hint of) assurance for the righteous (Q7:35); and
- good deeds will count ten times to one's credit while a bad deed will count "with its equivalent" (Q6:160).

I also noted passages that are similar to Jesus' story about Lazarus and the rich man in Luke 16:19–31: those in hell are seen by those in paradise, and the believers in paradise are unable to give the requested reprieves to the punished (Q42:44–46; 7:50–51). In Q7:163 we learn that God tempts the disbelieving people to break the Sabbath by causing fish to surface "only on [the Sabbath], never on weekdays". Another similar type of action on God's part is mentioned in Q6:42–45 where disbelievers are given prosperity by God, and

> ... as they revelled in what they had been given, we struck them suddenly and they were dumbfounded (Q6:44)

(Parallel verses can be found in Q7:94–96).

The only purpose I can think of for God needing to tempt people with fish or bring them prosperity before exacting judgment is that deeds in Islam have a weightier significance than mere belief or faith. If God can bring out their wickedness that shows their disbelief, He can, perhaps more justifiably, display his wrath. As a critique of this process of God bringing about his just wrath—if suffering and affluence do not prove God's existence, as the unbelievers reasoned, "hardship and affluence also befell our forefathers" (Q7:95), then why is God's punishment in these cases just?

The third development I found in these third-period Meccan *suras* is in the way that Muhammad is portrayed. While he is still the warner he has maintained himself to be (Q46:9), it appears that he thought of himself as only sent to the Arabs (Q35:23–24), and not necessarily "the seal of the prophets" that Muslims believe him to be today (the greatness of his prophethood, though, is more developed in the Medinan *suras*).

Another interesting feature is that on several occasions the Qur'an suggests that Muhammad had not previously heard of the stories that were revealed to him; for example, those concerning Noah (Q11:49) and Joseph (Q12:3). Note that these stories also occur in the Bible.

Reflections on the *Suras* from Medina
2, 98, 64, 62, 8, 47, 3, 61, 57, 4, 65, 59, 33, 63, 24, 58, 22, 48, 66, 60, 110, 49, 9, 5

The Medinan *suras* provide yet further distinction and development in the message as revealed to Muhammad. These can be summed up under three main categories:

- specific messages about current battles and fighting in the way of God;
- the development of Muhammad's message at the level of an initiation of a complete religion instead of a mere warning to turn away from polytheism; and
- a further development in nature of the prophethood of Muhammad.

The *suras* that mention battles include: *Sura* 8 (battle of Badr), *Sura* 47, *Sura* 3 (battle of Badr and Uhud), *Sura* 59, *Sura* 33 (Battle of the Trench), *Sura* 48, and *Sura* 9 (preparations for the expeditions to Tabuk). Many interesting specific instructions are given in these Medinan *suras*:

- fighting during the fasting month is prohibited (Q2:217);
- but Muhammad leaves it ambiguous whether one can take part in killing when persecution is involved (Q2:217, cf. v.191);
- believers can "incur the wrath of God" in hell if they flee from a disbeliever while in battle (Q8:16);
- struggling for God's cause is listed as one ingredient for inheriting God's forgiveness (Q8:74);

- "fighting in God's way" involves killing other people (Q4:92–94) and is not merely an inner fight of oneself against sin as peaceful Muslims interpret *jihad*;
- there is a "high rank" and "tremendous reward" for those who take part in "striving in God's way" (Q4:95–96);
- from the context of Q4:95, "striving in God's way" and "fighting in God's way" seem synonymous;
- while in battle, God does not protect those who pray—instructions are given to have some stand guard while others pray (Q4:101–103).

The development of Muhammad's revelations to include instructions about proper conduct and true worship in this period of revealed *suras* point to a shift in Muhammad's message from a mere warning against polytheism to the establishment of an identifiable, organized religion. *Sura 2* particularly parallels Jesus' Sermon on the Mount (Matt 5–7) and Moses' instructions on various procedures for the Israelites in Deuteronomy. *Sura 2* speaks of the direction of prayer (vv. 142–149), fasting (vv. 183–187), fighting (vv. 190–194, 216–218), pilgrimage (vv. 196–203), suffering (vv. 214–215), gambling (vv. 219–220), orphans (v. 220), marriage with disbelievers (v. 221), menstruation (v. 222), sex (v. 223), taking oaths (vv. 224–227), divorce (vv. 228–232), breastfeeding (v. 233), widows (v. 234), refugees (v. 243), and giving (vv. 261–281). Similarly, in providing specific instruction about daily life, *Suras 4* and *5* also give instructions for proper living for believers. A second way that the Medinan *suras* develop Islam as a religion is that they focus more on who is a "true believer" and who is not, especially among Jews and Christians (Q62:6; 3:75ff; 3:199–200).

A third development in the Medinan *suras* is in the progress of the prophethood of Muhammad and his connection with God as the object of people's faith and belief (for example, Q9:61–99; 5:81,92). We see here a clear shift away from Muhammad being merely one of the prophets, specifically, one sent to Arab people as mentioned in the third Meccan period passage Q35:23–24. Muhammad orders his followers not to raise their voices above his or "your [good] deeds may be cancelled out" (Q49:2). He could have access to specific women who were related to him or his slaves, while other believers could not (Q33:50–52) ("lawful to you," a sexual permission?). Further, Muhammad is "more protective towards the believers than they are themselves" (Q33:6).

His wives are the mothers of believers (Q33:6) and will receive a double reward if they are "obedient to God and His Messenger and [do] good deeds" (Q33:31). Contributions of some may bring them closer to the prayers of Muhammad and thereby, to God's mercy (Q9:99). Muhammad is described not only as concerned for his people, but full of mercy (Q9:128), an attribute that makes one question its relevancy if God's mercy is really the only thing that should matter to the believers. Furthermore, "God and his messenger" may make decisions together which are to be undisputed (Q33:36).

Among the interesting verses in this section, which are too numerous to list here, I was surprised to read a prohibition against eating food sacrificed to idols as in Q5:3. One of the critiques of Muhammad's reforms in Arab society is that he employed near syncretistic practices in order to win the masses. The *hajj*, for example, was a pagan practice from before his time. The worship around the *kaba* was another polytheistic practice. Yet some of Muhammad's revelations did strictly separate believers from polytheists, and the case mentioned in Q5:3 is even more strict than the Christian teaching on this topic (1 Cor 8:4, 8). Another example of the Qur'an diverting from syncretistic practices is mentioned in M.A.S. Abdel Haleem's introduction to *Sura* 58, where Muhammad instigates a prohibition against a pagan divorce practice.

HOW THE QUR'AN CAME TO BE

Dr Anthony McRoy[1]

Introduction

There is frequently a cleavage between the religious believer and the historian, notably when it comes to the origin of the former's religion. Usually, religion involves the supernatural. The historian studies the natural, and adopts a generally agnostic approach to supernatural matters—certainly, to matters of divine revelation. That is, he neither affirms nor denies them. Rather, he simply examines the circumstances in which divine revelation is said to have occurred.

Regarding Christianity, and more specifically the Gospels, the task of the historian is arguably easier. No one claims that Jesus wrote the Gospels Himself, nor "dictated" them the way YHWH is said to have dictated the Decalogue. Rather, the traditional claim is that His apostles (specifically Matthew and John) or members of apostolic teams (such as Mark, who had been in both Paul's and Peter's team, and Luke, who was in Paul's team), wrote the Gospels under the protection of the Holy Spirit (although liberal scholars challenge part or all of this). The traditional view of the Early Church is that Matthew wrote the first Gospel, as stated by Papias (c. 70–155, *Exposition of the Oracles of the Lord,* preserved by Eusebius, died c. 339): "Matthew put together the oracles [of the Lord] in the Hebrew dialect [i.e. Aramaic], and each one interpreted them as best he could."

However, most modern scholars hold that Mark was written first, and then was adapted by Matthew and Luke. One possibility that several have held is that Papias is referring to the tradition that Matthew took notes in Aramaic as Jesus spoke and acted, and these

---

[1] Dr McRoy, of dual UK\Eire nationality is a lecturer in Islamic Studies at Union School of Theology in Wales and author and contributor to several books. He is married with three adult children.

were later used by the Evangelists as one of their sources (Zahn, 1917: 408). The point is, the different proposed solutions to the Synoptic Problem can be held by either conservatives or liberals, or even atheists.

It is otherwise when we come to Islam. Essentially, the Islamic view of inspiration is one where dictation is indeed involved. Furthermore, whereas Early Church figures such as Papias, Irenaeus (c. 180), Eusebius, *et al*, are all important historical witnesses to how the Gospels emerged, no Christian grants any such post-apostolic writers the status of revelation in any form. As human beings *un*-guarded by the Holy Spirit, it was indeed possible for them to err.

However, the major source for the history of the revelation and compilation of the Qur'an, viewed as the word of Allah, is the hadith corpus[2]. In Islam it is granted a sort of secondary inspiration—seen as the word of the Prophet (and sometimes, for Sunnis, that of his *Sahaba*—the "Companions," Muhammad's close associates—or for Shia, the *Imams*—Muhammad's progeny through Ali). This is purportedly based on *Sura Ahzab* 33:21—that Muhammad is the pattern for Muslims. The historian faces two problems here: Sunnis and Shia have distinct, sometimes competing and mutually contradictory hadith collections—including on this subject. Furthermore, the hadith corpus was only collected around two centuries after the events it portrays.

1. Emergence of the Qur'an

The Qur'an, unlike the Bible, is not largely a narrative history, except normally when it is utilising biblical/apocryphal material, as with the cycles of Abraham, Noah, etc. Hence, this makes it difficult to present an historical setting for an event. For example, the beginning of the ministry of John the Baptist is given temporal location in Luke 3:1–2 (ESV):

> *In the fifteenth year of the reign of Tiberius Caesar, Pontius Pilate being governor of Judea, and Herod being tetrarch of Galilee, and his brother Philip tetrarch of the region of Ituraea and Trachonitis, and Lysanias tetrarch of Abilene, during the high priesthood of*

---

[2] Ed. There are several collections of the hadith. The most famous and well recognised is *Sahih Al-Bukhari*.

> *Annas and Caiaphas, the word of God came to John the son of Zechariah in the wilderness.*

Even if the timing is not so specific, when it comes to the Sermon on the Mount (in Luke's Gospel), we are informed as to the circumstances:

> *In these days he went out to the mountain to pray ... And when day came, he called his disciples and chose from them twelve, whom he named apostles ... And he came down with them and stood on a level place, with a great crowd of his disciples and a great multitude of people from all Judea and Jerusalem and the seacoast of Tyre and Sidon ... And he ... said: "Blessed are you who are poor, for yours is the kingdom of God."* (Luke 6:12–13, 17, 20)

Thus, the Gospel record gives us *context* for the saying and action. Luke tells us that others had written before him, and that he had consulted eyewitnesses (1:1–4), so he probably wrote Luke–Acts by 70 A.D. The so-called *Epistle of Clement*, (a letter from the elders of the church at Rome to that of Corinth), written c. 95, quotes Luke 6.38 in *1 Clement* 13; Acts 13:22 is quoted in *1 Clement* 18:1, showing that Luke–Acts had been written by 95, and had circulated around the Roman Empire, as a letter from Italy to Greece would suggest. Further, we have two important witnesses from the mid-second century about Luke's work: The *Anti-Marcionite Prologue* (Rome, c. 160–180), which informs us that Luke "wrote down this gospel in the parts of Achaia ... And indeed afterwards the same Luke wrote the Acts of the Apostles." *The Muratorian Canon* (Rome, c. 170) states: "The third book of the Gospel is that according to Luke."

Thus, the historian can be assured of an early date for the text he is reading—clearly Luke–Acts was written in the same century as the events it records. This gives us greater confidence about the context it supplies for those events. Further, Luke–Acts is not the product of state-supported or directed propaganda; rather, as the two-volume work displays, the followers of Jesus were often subject to persecution. The dating is thus essential—if Luke and/or his sources were simply inventing a tale, there would have been opponents still around who were often in a position of power, and thus able to challenge what was presented.

It is at this point we turn to the emergence of the Qur'an. Among the earliest texts was the *Sirah*, a biography of Muhammad by Ibn Ishaq who died in 761—that is, around 130 years after the events it portrays. It only survives in part, through the work of Ibn Hisham, who died c. 833, meaning that the extant work is even further removed from the actual events. Moreover, unlike the hadith[3], it is *not* viewed as religiously canonical. Perhaps ninety per cent of Muslims are Sunni, so we will look first at what the Sunni Hadith tells us:

> Sahih Al-Bukhari Hadith 1.3
> Narrated by Aishah
> *The commencement of the (Divine) Revelation to Allah's Messenger ... He used to go in seclusion in the cave of Hira' ... The angel came to him and asked him to read. The Prophet replied, "I do not know how to read." The Prophet ... added, "Then the angel caught me (forcefully) and pressed me so hard that I could not bear it any more ... Thereupon he caught me for the third time and pressed me, and then released me and said, 'Read in the Name of your Lord, Who has created (all that exists). Has created man from a clot (a piece of thick coagulated blood). Read! And your Lord is the Most Generous.'" (cf. Q96:1–3) Then Allah's Messenger returned with the Revelation and with his heart beating severely ...* (Khan, 1, 1997: 46–47)

Clearly, it is beyond the ability of the historian, employing what are essential secular tools, to question the veracity of the angelic appearance in the text, beyond noting perhaps that there are no external witnesses to the purported event, as the text states that Muhammad was in "seclusion". The most an historian could say is that this is the Sunni tradition concerning the emergence of the Qur'an. There are, however, several historiographical problems associated with it. Firstly, this is a *Sunni* narration, rather than being a *common* Islamic tradition. Secondly, Bukhari died in 870, yet his Hadith collection purportedly presents an authoritative report of the life and sayings of Muhammad, who perished in 632 according to Muslim sources. There is thus a problem of *temporal separation* between the supposed narration or action and its *written record*.

This is further complicated by the problem of *extant* copies of Bukhari's corpus. The earliest extant fragment of the *Sahih* consists of only three chapters (Melchert, 2010: 446). Mingana

---

[3] Ed. The Hadith are the sayings of the Prophet Muhammad that are not found in the Qur'an though on many occasions they are commentaries or explanations of quranic material. .

dated the manuscript to c.1000 A.D. (Mingana, 1936: 287). The basis for contemporary copies of the *Sahih* only go back to the fourteenth century A.D.:

> *Only versions of Firabri's recension, not even the recension of Nasafi as well, were available to al-Yunini (d. 701/1302), whose work formed the textual basis of the so-called Sultani edition of 1311–1313 (mid-1890s), the main basis in turn of subsequent editions and the closest we have to a standard text today.* (Melchert, 2010: 446)

Thus, the gap between the supposed event which led to the emergence of the Qur'an and its written record is two hundred years, and somewhat more if we consider the extant manuscripts of Bukhari. Hence, it is not easy for the historian to accept that a man in seventh-century Arabia arrived home one night claiming an angel visited him. The atheist may discount the very possibility of an angelic encounter, but the historian's problem is that the evidence for the assertion is so late that he must be sceptical about even whether the man ever *claimed* that in the first place.

The reader will have noted the reference in the Hadith 1.3 to *Sura Al-Alaq* (96:1–3): "Read: In the name of thy Lord who createth, Createth man from a clot. Read: And thy Lord is the Most Bounteous" (Pickthall translation). There is no gap in theme from the subsequent two verses: "Who teacheth by the pen, Teacheth man that which he knew not." The whole *Sura* consists of nineteen verses. None of them provide an historical context for any part of the chapter. Reynolds notes that neither traditional Muslims nor traditional Western scholars "conclude that the story of Muhammad's call might have been written as a way of explaining Q96:1–5, which would mean that explaining these verses through the story of Muhammad's call would be problematic, to say the least" (Reynolds, 2008: 9).

However, surely the objective historian is not meant to be a theologian; he must follow the evidence where it leads him. Is there any compelling historical evidence from the seventh century to regard *Sura Al-Alaq* as being the consequence of that initial encounter at Mount Hira, or is it rather the case that the hadith reflects a later tradition seeking to utilise the verse in a constructed —and possibly artificial—history? To illustrate, consider the NT Apocrypha. Essentially, it fills in gaps in the Gospel record—what did the infant Jesus do in Egypt, etc. Whereas the biblical Jesus does not begin His miracles until an adult, in these infancy gospels, His miraculous powers are already at work, as in the fifth century *Gospel of Pseudo-Matthew*, chapter 20, depicting Mary in the desert during the flight into Egypt:

> ... she looked up to the foliage of the palm, and saw it full of fruit, and said to Joseph: I wish it were possible to get some of the fruit of this palm ... Then the child Jesus ... said to the palm: O tree, bend thy branches, and refresh my mother with thy fruit. And immediately at these words the palm bent its top down to the very feet of the blessed Mary ... Then Jesus said to it: ... open from thy roots a vein of water which has been hid in the earth, and let the waters flow ... And it rose up immediately, and at its root there began to come forth a spring of water ...

A redacted form of this story is found in *Sura Maryam*, 19:22–26, with Joseph omitted, no reference to the flight into Egypt, and Mary still pregnant with Jesus. It is important to recall how *little* is stated in the Gospel (of Matthew, chap 2) about the flight:

> ... an angel of the Lord appeared to Joseph in a dream and said, "Rise, take the child and his mother, and flee to Egypt ..." And he rose and took the child and his mother by night and departed to Egypt and remained there until the death of Herod ... (Matthew 2:13–15, ESV)

Clearly, the Apocryphal text answers the urge to know more about the flight. This problem is accentuated when we come to the Qur'an, as there is not the same degree of narrative and biography we find in the Gospels, but people needed to know how Muhammad was called to be a Prophet, and how the holy text was revealed. Thus, it could be argued that the Hadith answered this need by *creating* a context for the emergence of the Qur'an around *Sura 96*. The difference is, post-biblical texts such as the *Gospel of Pseudo-Matthew* were never recognised as canonical, whereas the Hadith is so.

There is a further problem—there is no Islamic consensus at what happened when Muhammad was called to prophethood. The Shia agree that Muhammad was called at Mount Hira, but diverge thereafter. Specifically, according to the Sunni tradition, Muhammad was frightened and confused as to what was happening to him, so his wife Khadijah brought him to her cousin Waraqa, a Christian scribe, who surmised that he had experienced an angelic encounter and was called to prophethood. This is rejected by Shia, since Waraqa never converted; there are multiple and varying versions of the story; and because such a situation was theologically impossible, according to Qādi 'Ayyād (d. 1149): *"Certainly the matter (of revelation) was always clear for him,* because Divine wisdom necessitates that the matter should become completely clear for him" (Jaffer, 2009: 37, emphasis author's).

Two further problems arise as to the emergence of the Qur'an: that of external witnesses, and archaeological evidence. Certainly, there are no surviving Hijazi Arab, Christian, Jewish, Zoroastrian or pagan documents from the purported time of Muhammad's calling and subsequent initial proclamation of the Qur'an—if any did exist. Neither do we find anything about the Qur'an in the earliest non-Muslim sources, e.g. the *Doctrina Jacobi*, dated 634, written by a Jew who had been forcibly baptised: "When [Sergius] the *candidatus* was killed by the Saracens ... we Jews were overjoyed. And they were saying, 'A prophet has appeared, coming with the Saracens and he is preaching the arrival of the anointed one who is to come, the Messiah ...' 'In fact, he says that he has the keys of paradise, which is impossible'" (Shoemaker, 2012: 22–23).

Note the purported *kerygma* (message) here: the Prophet engages in the eschatological proclamation of the Messiah—possibly a reference to the Second Coming—and claims to control entrance to heavenly rewards. Yet there is nothing about the Qur'an. It is often said that the Qur'an holds the position in Islam (especially in Sunnism) that Jesus holds in Christianity, so perhaps we could expect some reference to it. After all, Josephus (a Jew) and Tacitus (a pagan), two of the earliest non-Christian commentators on Christianity, seemed to understand the centrality of Jesus for the Christian *kerygma*. If the essence of Islam is the Qur'an and its doctrine, it is surprising that nothing of this is mentioned in the early non-Muslim witnesses. The nearest reference is found in the Armenian work of Sebeos, c.660s,[4] referring to Muhammad: "He legislated (*awrinadre*) for them not to eat carrion (v.3), not to drink wine (ii.219, v.90), not to speak falsely (xxxix.3, xvi.116, xxxiii.24 etc.) and not to commit fornication (xvii.32, xxiv.2)" (Hoyland, 1997:131). However, as Hoyland notes, "Sebeos makes no reference to Muhammad bearing a

---

[4] Ed. The usually accepted dates for Muhammad's life are c570 – 632AD.

scripture." Apart from the insistence on teetotalism, the injunctions are not distinctive—essentially those found in the Bible.

Another issue is archaeological. The oldest extant Muslim building is Jerusalem's Dome of the Rock, completed in 691. The calligraphy therein agrees somewhat with the Qur'an, but not wholly. For example, in the Inner Octagon, we find this call, absent from the Qur'an, referring to Muhammad: "The blessing of Allah be on him and peace be on him, and may Allah have mercy." Another sentence, referring to Jesus, states: "Peace be on him the day he was born, and the day he dies, and the day he shall be raised alive!" This looks like *Sura Maryam* 19.33 ("Peace on me the day I was born, and the day I die, and the day I shall be raised alive!") but note the change from first to third person. The exact wording corresponds to Q19.15 ("Peace on him the day he was born, and the day he dieth and the day he shall be raised alive,") where it refers *not* to Jesus, but to *John the Baptist*. Why take a verse referring to John and apply it to Jesus?

Again, on the Outer Octagon, we find a blessing on Muhammad: "the blessing of Allah be on him. May He accept his intercession on the Day of Judgment on behalf of his people." It is also an idea that is absent from the Qur'an, and only found in the Hadith (Sahih Al-Bukhari 8.317B). This may suggest that the Hadith borrowed the idea from the Dome. On the Dome's Copper Plaques, we find Allah called "the Pillar of the heavens and the earth"—a description absent from the Qur'an. There is a reference to "all sovereignty belongs to You and is from You," which is also not in the Qur'an. Space does not allow for a list of other discrepancies, but we may ask the question—was the Qur'anic text not yet stabilised? Consider various contemporary religious or commemorative monuments, e.g. to the "Glorious Dead" of the Great War. Often these include biblical quotes (specifically from the Authorised Version). Certainly, the architects and builders would be sure to make certain that their quotations were correct, so how do we explain the discrepancies on the Dome?

2.   Compilation of the Qur'an

Further questions arise when we turn to how the Qur'an was compiled. There are two Sunni traditions about how the revelations given to Muhammad were collated:

Sahih Al-Bukhari 6.201

4679. Narrated Zaid bin Thabit Al-Ansāri ...:
Abu Bakr sent for me after the (heavy) casualties among the warriors (of the battle) of Yamāma [where a great number of Qurra' (those who know the Qur'an by heart) were killed]. 'Umar was present with Abu Bakr who said, "Umar has come to me and said, 'The people have suffered heavy casualties on the day of (the battle of) Yamāma, and I am afraid that there will be more casualties among the Qurra' at other battlefields, whereby a large part of the Qur'an may be lost, unless you collect it ...'" Abu Bakr added, "I said to 'Umar, 'How can I do something which Allah's Messenger ... has not done?' ... Abu Bakr said (to me), "You ... used to write the Divine Revelation for Allah's Messenger ... Therefore, look for the Qur'an and collect it (in one manuscript)." ... So, I started to search for the Qur'anic material and to collect it from parchments, scapula, leafstalks of date palms and from the memories of men (who knew it by heart) ... The manuscript on which the Qur'an was collected, remained with Abu Bakr till Allah took him unto Him, and then with 'Umar till Allah took him unto Him, and finally it remained with Hafsa, 'Umar's daughter. (Khan, 1, 1997: 156–157)

According to this, the Qur'an existed in fragmentary form in Muhammad's lifetime, and was only collated because of an emergency. It was collected under state direction by Zaid ibn Thabit during the reign of the first Caliph, Abu Bakr in 633. However, another tradition has the same individual replicating his actions under 'Uthman, 653:

Sahih Al-Bukhari 6.510
4987. Narrated Anas bin Malik
... Hudhaifa was afraid of their (the people of Sham and 'Iraq) differences in the recitation of the Qur'an ... So 'Uthmān sent a message to Hafsa saying, "Send us the manuscript of the Qur'an so that we may compile the Qur'anic materials in perfect copies and return the manuscript to you." Hafsa sent it to 'Uthmān. 'Uthmān then ordered Zaid bin Thābit, 'Abdullāh bin Az-Zubair, Sa'id bin Al-'As and 'Abdur-Rabman bin Harith bin Hishām to copy the (original) manuscript perfectly. 'Uthman said to the three Quraishi men, "In case you disagree with Zaid bin Thabit on any point in the Qur'an, then write it in the dialect of Quraish as the Qur'an was revealed in their tongue." They did so, and when they had written many copies, 'Uthmān returned the original manuscripts to Hafsa. 'Uthmān sent to every Muslim province one copy of what they had copied, and ordered that all the other Qur'anic materials, whether written in fragmentary manuscripts or whole copies, be burnt.
(Khan, 6, 1997: 425–426)

The tradition alludes to the possibility that the three Quraishi men might have disagreed with Zaid. It states that 'Uthman not only sent several copies to the provinces, but ordered the destruction of all existing Qur'ans save for the one of Hafsa. Why this distribution did not occur under Abu Bakr is not stated. At this point, textual criticism is useful. It used to be claimed that the Topkapi and Tashkent manuscripts were from 'Uthman, but a study by two Turkish scholars found that the Topkapi did not go back to 'Uthman, but was rather dated to the Umayyad period, 661–750 (Altıkulaç, and İhsanoğlu, 2007: 80–81). Neither did the Tashkent copy go back to 'Uthman (ibid.: 67). There seems to be no extant manuscripts that go back to 'Uthman. The parchment of the Birmingham Mingana manuscript, which elicited notice in 2015, was radiocarbon dated to between AD 568 and 645, but that only tells us when the animal from whose skin it was made was alive (University of Birmingham, 2015). However, the *ink* was not subjected to the study, and no palaeographical examination has yet been made or released to determine the age of the script.

Further, it does not appear that competing Qur'anic manuscripts *were* all destroyed as ordered by the Caliph. The *Fihrist* of Ibn al-Nadim (died c. 995), a listing of Arabic books, refers to the *Mushafs* of Ibn Mas'ud, which excluded *Suras* 1, 113 and 114 and was in a different order to that of 'Uthman; and of Ubayy bin Ka'b, which contained two extra *suras* and was also ordered differently (Dodge, 1970: 57–62). We also know of that of Ibn 'Abbas, which also had two extra *suras* and was also ordered differently (von Denffer, 1983: 49f). Interestingly, a parallel hadith to Al-Bukhari 6.510 confirms resistance to the destruction order:

> Jämi' at-Tirmidhi Vol. 5, (19). 3104.
> ... *Az-Zuhri said: "'Ubaidullāh bin 'Abdullāh bin 'Utbah informed me that 'Abdullāh bin Mas'ud disliked Zaid bin Thābit copying the Musāhif, and he said: 'O you Muslim people! Avoid copying the Mushaf and recitation of this man. By Allah! When I accepted Islam he was but in the loins of a disbelieving man'—meaning Zaid bin Thābit—and it was regarding this that 'Abdullāh bin Mas'ud d said: 'O people of Al-'Iraq! Keep the Musāhif that are with you, and conceal them. For indeed Allah said: And whoever conceals something, he shall come with what he concealed on the Day of Judgement. So meet Allah with the Musāhif.'"* ... (Abu Khaliyl, 2007: 412, 414)

The first (known) Greek translation of the Qur'an was in the ninth century, under Nicetas of Byzantium in his *Refutatio* (he may have used a translator). What is interesting is that it excluded *Sura* 1, and sometimes agreed with the readings of Ibn 'Abbas (Versteegh, 1991: 62–64). The first question is where the translator got this text—especially considering that as a Byzantine, he was a subject of the great enemy state of the Caliphate—and secondly, why did it contain so many variants, given that 'Uthman ordered the destruction of all previous Qur'anic manuscripts (Veestegh mentions a number of other variants)? Is this a sign of the fluidity of the Qur'anic text in the ninth century?

This may be strengthened by the nature of the Sana'a codex, discovered in 1972. Deroche observes its difference from the standard so-called 'Uthmanic type:

> *At the more general level of variation, the order of the suras differs from the standard text: s. 8 comes after s. 11, s. 19 after s. 9, s. 18 after s. 12, s. 25 after s. 15, s. 13 after s. 34, s. 62 after s. 63 and s. 89 after s. 62.51 As noted by Sadeghi and Goudarzi, there is a broad agreement with Ubayy's codex ... Other Qur'anic manuscripts found in Sanaa similarly reveal a different sequence of the suras.* Deroche, 2014: 52)

Deroche dates the codex to "the second half of the first/seventh century and erased at the earliest by the middle of the following century" (ibid.: 54). What is particularly significant for this study is that sometimes Sana'a codex agreed with the text of Ibn Mas'ud, sometimes with that of Ubayy, and was sometimes independent.

The historian may ask at this point, given the evidence of the Sana'a codex and Nicetas of Byzantium's translation, whether the supposed order from 'Uthman is historical or actually read back by later authorities? Were there different traditions that ascribed the collation to 'Uthman and then to Abu Bakr, which were then subsequently fused together? This is where redaction criticism becomes valuable, even more so since there may have been a polemical reason for the different traditions—the Sunni–Shia divide. According to the Shia, the Qur'an was *already* fully written down in the lifetime of Muhammad—by his son-in-law Ali:

> Usul al-Kafi H 607, Ch. 35, h 1
> Muhammad ibn Yahya has narrated from Ahmad ibn Muhammad from ibn Mahbub from 'Amr ibn abu al-

Miqdam from Jabir who has said that he heard abu Ja'far (a.s.) say the following.
No one from the people has claimed to have collected the whole of the Holy Quran (in a book form) as it was revealed. If anyone would come up with such a claim, he is liar. No one collected this Holy Book and memorized as Allah, the Most Holy, the Most High revealed it except Ali ibn abu Talib (a.s.) and the Imams after him. (Sarwar, 1999: 450)

Usul al-Kafi H Vol. 8 14452
Muhammad Bin Ali Bin Ma'mar, from Muhammad Bin Ali Bin Ukaayat Al-Tamimy, from Al-Husayn Bin Al-Nazar Al-Fahry, from Abu Amro Al-Awzaiy, from Amro Bin Shimr, from Jabir Bin Yazeed who said:
I came up to Abu Ja'far (as), so I said, O son of the Messenger of Allah, the differing among the Shi'ites in this Doctrine causes me pain. He (as) said: Listen attentively and make it reach to wherever your ride takes you, that Amir-ul-Momineen (as) preached to the people at Al-Medina seven days after the passing away of the Messenger of Allah, and that was when he was free from collecting the Quran and compiling it ... (HubeAli, n.d.: 25)

These texts indicate that the collation of the Qur'an occurred under Ali, while Muhammad was yet alive, as Shia writers insist:

> *Ibn al-Nad'im, al-Ya'qubi and many Shi'i traditionists have mentioned the episode of the compilation of the Qur'an by 'Ali (A) after the Prophet's demise. The arrangement of the surahs in 'Ali's mushaf, as mentioned by al-Ya'qubi in his history, is different from those of Ibn Mas'ud and Ubayy ibn Ka'b, which have been described by Ibn al Nadim. There are minor differences also in the names of the surahs from the well-known and presently popular names.* (Shanehchi, 1943: 4)

So, this edition of the Qur'an also differed in order. Shia tradition (*Kafi*, Vol. 2: 633) states that Ali's edition was offered to the Sahaba (companions of the Prophet), but was rejected, and that when the Qaim (Mahdi) comes, he will restore the Alid Qur'an:

> In *Kafi* it is reported from Salim bin Abi Salma that he said:
> *I heard a man read out a portion of Qur'an to His Eminence, Abi Abdullah Sadiq (as) in way that was absolutely different from the manner it is recited. So His Eminence, Abu Abdullah (as) told him not to recite it like that. He urged him to read it in the usual way that people generally read till the reappearance of the Qaim (aj). Thus when His Eminence, Qaim reappears he will recite the Book of Allah according to its rules and he will bring out a copy of Qur'an*

> *inscribed by Ali (as). Then he said: "When Ali (as) completed writing it and became free after its compilation he took it out to the people saying: "This is the Book of Allah, the Mighty and Sublime as Allah revealed it upon His Eminence, Muhammad. Indeed, I have compiled it from two tablets." The people said: "We have a compiled copy with us and we do not need this (your) copy." He said: "By Allah, after this day, you will not see it ever. It was only incumbent on me to inform you after I have compiled it, so that you may read it.* (Isfahani, 2008: 112)

Hence, there is no consensus on the date of the compilation of the Qur'an, or its order.

Conclusion

Given the lack of manuscript evidence, and the absence of reference to the Qur'an in the earliest reports, can we speculate on how it emerged? There seems no reason to doubt that a man claiming to be a Prophet claimed "revelations," which contained predictive, ethical and ritual elements—but how developed and extensive were these, and were they written down in his lifetime—or shortly after? After he died, were there competing claims about what he said? The difficulty is that Muhammad's "revelations" were accompanied by "holy war" and thus state power—and direction. How much of the Qur'an is the result of political imposition? Traditionalist and Revisionist scholars offer different hypotheses.

One issue deserving attention is the extent of Qur'anic reliance on previous religious writings—notably Old Testament and New Testament Apocrypha. Specifically, applying the disciplines of Source and Redaction Criticism to *Sura Maryam* and some other *ayat*, we find dependence upon, and editing of Infancy of Jesus apocrypha, e.g. the *Protoevangelium of James*, dated to the late second century, emanating from Syria; as we have seen, the *Gospel of Pseudo-Matthew*, dated late fifth century, and dependent on the former and also on the second century *Gospel of Thomas the Israelite*, which we know from a sixth century manuscript existed in Syriac. Syriac Christians—Jacobites (Miaphysite) and Nestorians—existed in Arabia, notably in the tribal confederacies allied to Byzantium—the Jacobite Ghassanids—and on the Persian side, the Nestorian Lakhmids.

It has long been noted that there is great Syriac linguistic influence in the Qur'an (Mingana, 1927: 78–79). For example, the fact that the Qur'an calls Jesus *'Isa,* which is probably derived from the Eastern Syriac (i.e. Nestorian) *Isho* (Robinson, 1991: 19). Mingana also notes "apocryphal books circulating among the members of the Syrian Churches of South Syria and Arabia," and that "the majority of the Christians round about Hijaz and South Syria belonged to the Jacobite community" (Mingana, 1927: 80, 83).

The period around the emergence of Muhammad's movement was a time of military conflict between Byzantium and Persia, with the former's Emperor, Heraclius, inventing the concept of Christian holy war and *military* martyrdom, as well as trying—and failing—to resolve the Chalcedonian–Miaphysite split through Christological innovations such as Monoenergism (that Christ had one activity) and Monothelitism (one will), and eschatological speculation. In such ferment, we can comprehend the emergence of a nativistic Arab theology which employed a redacted form of apocryphal literature to distinguish itself from the Jewish and Christian Scriptures, and which offered a simplistic Unitarian Christology, along with an *Ur-Qur'an*, which later was developed and extended by the Umayyads. Of course, as with the Dead Sea Scrolls, if some Bedouin boy should one day come upon a cave with jars holding manuscripts demonstrably dated to the time of Muhammad, such speculation would end—but no such event has yet occurred.

Bibliography

Altıkulaç, Tayyar and İhsanoğlu, Edmeleddin, 2007, *Al-Muṣḥaf al-Sharīf Attributed to 'Uthmān bin 'Affān*, Istanbul: Organization of the Islamic Conference Research Centre for Islamic History, Art and Culture

von Denffer, Ahmed, 1983, *Ulum al-Quran*, Leicester: Islamic Foundation

Deroche, Francois, 2014, *Qur'ans of the Umayyads*, Leiden/Boston: Brill

Dodge, Bayard (trans.), 1970, *The Fihrist of al-Nadim*, Vol. I, New York & London: Columbia University Press

Hoyland, Robert G., 1997, *Seeing Islam as Others Saw It: A Survey and Evaluation of Christian, Jewish and Zoroastrian Writings on Early Islam*, Princeton: Darwin Press

HubeAli, *Al-Kafi*, Vol. 8, Part 1 (n.d. https://www.hubeali.com/alkafivol1/ cited 1 August, 2017

Isfahani, Ayatullah Muhammad Taqi Musawi, 2008, *Mikyalul Makarim Fee Fawaaid ad-Duaa Lil Qai'm vol. 1*, Mumbai: Ja'fari Propagation Centre

Jaffer, Abbas, Jaffer, Masuma, 2009, *Quranic Sciences*, London: ICAS Press

Khaliyl, Abu (trans.), 2007, *Jämi' At-Tirmidhi*, Vol. 1, Riyadh: Darussalam

Khan, Muhammad Muhsin (trans.), 1997, *The Translation of the Meanings of Sahîh Al-Bukhâri*, Vol. 1, Riyadh: Darussalam

Khan, Muhammad Muhsin (trans.), 1997, *The Translation of the Meanings of Sahîh Al-Bukhâri*, Vol. 6, Riyadh: Darussalam

Melchert, Christopher, 2010, 'Bukhārī and his *Ṣaḥīḥ*', *Le Muséon* 123 (3-4)

Mingana, A., 1927 'Syriac Influence on the Style of the Kur'an', *Bulletin of the John Rylands Library*, Manchester,

------------ 1936, 'An Important MS. of Bukhārī's Sahīh', *Journal of the Royal Asiatic Society of Great Britain & Ireland*, 68(2)

Reynolds, Gabriel Said, 2008, 'Introduction: Qur'anic studies and its controversies' in Reynolds, Gabriel Said (Ed.), *The Qur'an in its Historical Context*, London & New York: Routledge

Robinson, Neal, 1991, *Christ in Islam and Christianity*, London: Macmillan

Sarwar, Muhammad, 1999[?], *Al-Kafi*, Volume 1, Qom: Darolhadith Scientific-Cultural Institute

Shanehchi, Kazim Mudir, 1363 [1943], *Some Old Manuscripts of the Holy Qur'an*, https://www.al-islam.org/al-tawhid/vol-8-no4/some-old-manuscripts-holy-quran-kazim-mudir-shanehchi/some-old-manuscripts-holy cited 16 August, 2017

Shoemaker, Stephen J, 2012, *The Death of a Prophet: The End of Muhammad's Life and the Beginning of Islam*, Philadelphia: University of Pennsylvania Press

University of Birmingham, 'Birmingham Qur'an manuscript dated among the oldest in the world', 22. July 2015, http://www.birmingham.ac.uk/news/latest/2015/07/quran-manuscript-22-07-15.aspx cited 15 August, 2017

Versteegh, Kees, 1991, *'Greek Translations* of the Qur'an in Christian Polemics (9th century A.D.)', *Zeitschrift der Deutschen Morgenländischen Gesellschaft* Vol. 141, No. 1

Zahn, Theodor, 1917, *Introduction to the New Testament*, New York: Charles Scribner's Sons

THE CHALLENGE OF THE SANA'A MANUSCRIPTS TO THE MUSLIM CLAIM OF THE PERFECT QUR'AN[1]

Christina A. Cirucci M.D.[2]

Muslims believe that the Qur'an is the perfectly maintained record of the exact words of God as revealed to the Prophet Muhammad between 610 and 632 AD. In contradistinction to the Christian view of the Bible (that the Bible is the Word of God, inerrant in its *original* form), Muslims believe that the Qur'an is inerrant in its *current* form. Until recently, the oldest Qur'an manuscripts were dated not earlier than one hundred years after Muhammad's death or 732 AD.[3,4] In 1972, however, Qur'an manuscripts were found at a mosque in Sana'a, Yemen. The oldest of these manuscripts have been dated between 700 and 715 AD.[5] There are differences in the oldest Sana'a Qur'an and the Qur'an that is in use today, and although the differences do not change the principal meaning, the find is a challenge to the Muslim view that the Qur'an has been maintained exactly as it was given to Muhammad 1400 years ago.

In 1972, ancient parchments comprised of tens of thousands of fragments from almost a thousand different parchment codices of the Qur'an[6] were discovered during restoration of the Great Mosque in Sana'a, Yemen. The parchments were locked up until

---

[1] This article was originally printed in the *CSIOF Bulletin*, Issue 5, Nov 2012, pp21-27
[2] Student in Biblical Studies, Columbia International University, Columbia, SC
[3] John Gilchrist, *Jam'al-Quran: The Codification of the Qur'an Text* (Mondeor, South Africa: MERCSA, 1989) http://www.answering-islam.org/Gilchrist/Jam/chap7.html (accessed August 18, 2011)
[4] Ahmad Von Denffer, *Ulum al-Quran: An Introduction to the Sciences of the Qur'an* (Leicestershire, UK: The Islamic Foundation, 2007), p61.
[5] Gerd Puin, as quoted in "The Oldest Qur'anic Manuscripts" http://www.youtube.com/watch?v=iNdvsLh128Q (accessed August 9, 2011)
[6] Toby Lester. "What is the Koran?" *The Atlantic Monthly*, January 1999, http://www.theatlantic.com/issues/99jan/koran.htm (accessed August 14, 2011)

1979 when Qadhi Ismail al-Akwa', the president of the Yemeni Antiquities Authority, recruited German scholar Dr. Gerd Puin to preserve and examine the documents. Puin was later joined by his colleague from Saarland University, Hans-Caspar Graf von Bothmer. Although the Germans have since been denied further access to the original manuscripts, there is a complete microfilm copy in Germany. The account of the Sana'a manuscripts is well documented in Toby Lester's article, "What is the Koran?" published in the January 1999 issue of *The Atlantic Monthly*.[7]

The Sana'a manuscripts are likely older than any other extant Qur'an manuscripts. Four fragments containing the first and last chapters of the Qur'an contain architectural drawings of mosques which allows for precise dating of the manuscripts. Puin states, "Because of its drawings, because of the art-historical context, you can date this Qur'an very precisely to the time of Al-Walid. This is the reign between 705 and 715."[8] Carbon 14 testing dates some of the manuscripts to 645–690 AD.[9]

Puin claims that the Sana'a manuscripts contain differences compared to today's Qur'an consisting of different verse orderings, minor textual variants, and rare styles of orthography and artistic embellishment.[10] Puin states, "Such aberrations, although not surprising to textual historians, are troublingly at odds with the orthodox Muslims ..."[11] Additionally, the Sana'a manuscripts were written in a form of Arabic that has no vowel markings or distinguishing marks, which means that an individual word can have up to thirty different meanings. Puin claims that "The sheer existence of so many different possible readings would suggest that this text wasn't passed down word for word. The text isn't as stable as it seems in the Cairo version."[12] There are also differences in the

---

[7] Ibid.
[8] Gerd Puin, as quoted in "The Oldest Qur'anic Manuscripts" http://www.youtube.com/watch?v=iNdvsLh128Q (accessed August 9, 2011)
[9] Sujit Das. "Ancient Qur'anic Manuscripts of Sana'a and Divine Downfall" May 6, 2011
http://www.faithfreedom.org/articles/quran-koran/ancient-qur%e2%80%99anic-manuscripts-of-sana%e2%80%99a-and-divine-downfall/ (accessed August 9, 2011)
[10] Lester.
[11] Gerd Puin, as quoted in "Oldest Yemeni Quran differs from Uthman Quran today" http://www.youtube.com/watch?v=OLSEaPxePZc&playnext=1&list=PLBBB589C38BF5185E (accessed August 9, 2011).
[12] Ibid.

order of *suras* in the Sana'a manuscripts. Puin questions whether this means that most of the *suras* were not written down and put into approximately their final form during Muhammad's lifetime.[13]

Additionally, the Sana'a documents contain palimpsests, areas of parchment where the text was washed off and written over. Regarding the palimpsests, Dr. Patrick Sookhdeo states, "If the researchers are correct, particularly on dating, this suggests in fact that the Qur'an was not a single sought after, single entity that was fixed by 650 but actually developed much, much later; hence the overlaying of texts of written materials."[14] Dr. Christoph Heger states,

> *Why the older layer was wiped out cannot be said definitely until it can be read in detail ... Most probably the arrangement of the surahs was altered. And this hypothesis is corroborated by the fact that amongst the findings in Sanaa [sic] there are indeed Qur'ans with an arrangement of surahs different from the transmitted Qur'an.*[15]

The discovery of the Sana'a documents, their dating, and their textual variations from today's Qur'an are of monumental significance in challenging the Muslim belief that the Qur'an is incorruptible, completely preserved in its current form. Sujit Das states unequivocally that discovery of the Sana'a manuscripts:

> *scattered the orthodox Muslim belief that the Qur'an as it has reached us today is quite simply "the perfect, timeless, and unchanging Word of God." It means the Qur'an has been distorted, perverted, revised, modified and corrected, and textual alterations had taken place over the years purely by Human hands ... and the core belief of millions plus Muslims that the Qur'an is the eternal, unaltered word of God is now clearly visible as a great hoax, a totally downright falsehood.*[16]

---

[13] Gerd Puin, "Observations on Early Qur'an Manuscripts in Sana'a" In *What the Koran Really Says: Language, Text and Commentary*, by Ibn Warraq. (Amherst, NY: Promethius Books, 2002), p742.
[14] Patrick Sookhdeo, as quoted in "The Oldest Qur'anic Manuscripts" http://www.youtube.com/watch?v=iNdvsLh128Q (accessed August 14, 2011)
[15] Christoph Heger, "A Qur'an Palimpsest from the Sanaa Qur'ans" http://www.christoph-heger.de/palimpse.htm (accessed August 14, 2011)
[16] Sujit Das, "Ancient Qur'anic Manuscripts of Sana'a and Divine Downfall"

Although not all would state it as polemically as Das, clearly the findings pose a challenge to the Muslim belief about the Qur'an.

What is the Muslim response? Several months after Toby Lester's article, Dr. Muhammad Mohar Ali published a review.[17] His main refutation is that although Lester claims that the Sana'a documents have unconventional verse ordering and minor textual variants, not a single example of any of these were given.[18] He concludes that "Puin and Lester have simply attempted to make a mountain out of a mole [sic] on the basis of inadequate, inconclusive, unclear and unspecified evidence."[19] Most of Ali's article centres on challenging other orientalists whom Lester refers to in his article. Ali's refutation is not an adequate one: Lester's article was not meant to be a detailed article for manuscript scholars, but one addressed to the lay public.

One popular Muslim website refutes the dating of the Sana'a manuscripts.[20] The author points out that although von Bothmer dated Codex Sana'a DAM 20–33 to around 710–715 AD, this date was vehemently argued by Jonathan Bloom. He quotes Bloom as saying, "there is no scientific proof for von Bothmer's claim that the manuscript has been carbon dated to the Umayyad period, and a ninth-century date seems more likely on the basis of script."[21] Furthermore, the author states that the resemblance of some codices to the "Great Umayyad Qur'an" suggests that the "Great Umayyad Qur'an" may have served as a model.[22] Regarding differences in the order of the *suras* in the Sana'a manuscripts, the

---

[17] Muhammad Mohar Ali, *The Qur'an and the Latest Orientalist Assumptions: Being a Review of Toby Lester's Article: "What is the Koran?"* (Ipswich,UK: Jam'iat Ihyaa' Minhaaj Al-Sunnah, 1999).
[18] Ibid,pp 8–9.
[19] Ibid, p10.
[20] "The Qur'anic Manuscripts" http://www.islamic-awareness.org/Quran/Text/Mss/ (accessed August 14,2011).
[21] JM Bloom in "The Introduction of Paper to The Islamic Lands and The Development of The Illustrated Manuscript", *Muqarnas*, 2000, Volume XVII, pp. 22–23 (footnote 15) as quoted in http://www.islamic-awareness.org/Quran/Text/Mss/yem1f.html (accessed August 14, 2011)
[22] "Codex Sana'a DAM 01-29.2 – A Qur'anic Manuscript From 2nd Century of Hijra" http://www.islamic-awareness.org/Quran/Text/Mss/yem2a.html (accessed August 14, 2011)

author states, "Simple logic dictates that if a person or patron wished to copy or have copied a few or even many *surahs* for personal or public edification, he or they were not limited to copying *surahs* adjoining each other only."[23] The website provides a very academic and informative evaluation of some of the Sana'a manuscripts. It challenges some of the dates provided by von Bothmer and some of the *sura* ordering, but does not completely address the differences in text.

Muhammad Mustafa Al-A'zami also addresses Toby Lester's article on the Sana'a documents and claims that Lester's approach is purely academic, that of a "curious reporter filing an objective report" with no credentials to write on Islam except that he lived in Yemen and Palestine.[24] He compares Gerd Puin to a bookbinder who completes a magnificent binding of a mathematical text and therefore thinks he is a world authority on mathematics.[25] He claims that Puin has since denied most of the findings Lester ascribed to him.[26] Shortly after the publication of Lester's article in *The Atlantic*, Puin did indeed write a letter to al-Qadi Isma'il al-Akwah which was published in the Yemeni newspaper *ath-Thawra*. Al-A'zami translates part of Puin's letter as follows:

> *The important thing, thank God, is that these Yemeni Qur'anic fragments do not differ from those found in museums and libraries elsewhere, with the exception of details that do not touch the Qur'an itself, but are rather differences in the way words are spelled. This phenomenon is well-known ...*[27]

Al-A'zami states that "This deflates the entire controversy, dusting away the webs of intrigue that were spun around Puin's discoveries and making them a topic unworthy of further speculation."[28] It seems that Puin's letter was more an effort in

---

[23] "Codex Sana'a DAM 01-27.1 – A Qur'anic Manuscript from Mid-1st Century of Hijra"
http://www.islamic-awareness.org/Quran/Text/Mss/soth.html (accessed August 14, 2011).
[22] Muhammad Mustafa Al-A'zami, *The History of the Qur'anic Text From Revelation to Compilation: A Comparative Study with the Old and New Testaments* (Leicester, England: UK Islamic Academy, 2003), p4.
[25] Ibid., p4.
[26] Ibid., p11.
[27] Ibid., p12.
[28] Ibid.

diplomacy, however, rather than a retraction of his assertions. Al-A'zami states: "There will never be a discovery of a Qur'an, fragmented or whole, which differs from the consensus text circulating throughout the world. If it does differ then it cannot be regarded as Qur'an, because one of the foremost conditions for accepting anything as such is that it conform [sic] to the text used in Uthman's Mushaf."[29] The Muslim belief about the Qur'an precludes the option to even question it. Al-A'zami doesn't adequately address the challenge posed by the Sana'a manuscripts; he simply disregards the issue.

Hamza Andreas Tzortzis has also written an article addressing the claims of Puin that there are discrepancies in the Sana'a manuscripts.[30] Tzortzis states that the claims of Puin are "clearly far-fetched and totally untenable."[31] Regarding the claim that there are some differences in the numbering of '*ayahs* in some *suras*, Tzortzis states, "Such difference in the numbering of 'ayahs is acknowledged even by some classical Muslim scholars and it does not affect the text at all."[32] Regarding the palimpsests, Tzortzis states that palimpsests "do not suggest anything more than correction of mistakes omitted in the writing of the words in the first instance. It cannot be a proof in support of the theory of revision of evolution of the text unless an earlier copy of the Qur'an containing different words and expressions in the same place is shown to exist. This has not been found in the Sana'a manuscripts."[33] Tzortzis also states:

> *the conclusion that the surahs were not written down in their final form during the lifetime of the Prophet or that a Qur'an with a different ordering of the surahs was in circulation for a long time just because two or three sheets have been found where some surahs have been written in a different order, that is surahs from different places of the Qur'an in circulation have been put together, is hasty and untenable ...*[34]

---

[29] Ibid., p13.
[30] Hamza Andreas Tzortzis, "Dr. Puin and the 'Yemeni' Manuscripts: Taken from 'The Qur'an & The Orientalists' by Mohar Ali"
http://hamzatzortzis.blogspot.com/2008/07/dr-puin-yemeni-manuscripts.html
(accessed August 14, 2011)
[31] Ibid.
[32] Ibid.
[33] Ibid.
[34] Ibid.

Interestingly, Tzortzis points out that Puin claims in a number of the Sana'a manuscripts the letter *alif* is written in a different way, but doesn't address this issue. He concludes his article by saying, "The existence of a Qur'an with a different arrangement of the surahs or with what is called 'corrections' and 'revisions' cannot be cited as proof that such a Qur'an has ever been in use among the Muslims."[35] Once again, the issues are not totally addressed, but discarded as not possible.

The findings of the Sana'a manuscripts certainly present a challenge to the Muslim belief that the Qur'an of today is the perfect record of what was revealed to Muhammad. When confronted with the challenge of the Sana'a manuscripts most Muslims are not willing to address the specifics of textual criticism. The most academic discussion is found at www.islamic-awareness.org, and even this website does not address the discrepancies of the Sana'a manuscripts but only challenges the dating. To the Muslim, if an old manuscript is discovered that is different from the Qur'an of today, then by definition, this manuscript is not valid. The point is well said by F.E. Peters:

> *When old Biblical manuscripts, parchments or ancient Hindu manuscripts are discovered, Christian and Hindu scholars almost climb over each other's shoulder to gain an early access to them. Such findings cause great excitement to them. But sadly, no such excitement exists in Islam. Christians and Hindus are eager to see more and more light shed on the earliest manuscripts of their scriptures, while Muslims resist, often with strong determination.*[36]

Once evaluation of the Sana'a documents is completed, it likely will provide further challenge to the Muslim view that the Qur'an has been maintained perfectly since the revelation to Muhammad, but Muslims will struggle to even consider this a possibility.

Bibliography

---

[35] Ibid.
[36] As quoted by Sujit Das. "Ancient Qur'anic Manuscripts of Sana'a and Divine Downfall"

Al-A'zami, Muhammad Mustafa. 2003, *The History of the Qur'anic Text from Revelation to Compilation: A Comparative Study with the Old and New Testaments*, Leicester, England: UK Islamic Academy.

Ali, Muhammad Mohar. 1999, *The Qur'an and the Latest Orientalist Assumptions: Being a Review of Toby Lester's Article: "What is the Koran?"* Ipswich, UK: Jam'iat Ihyaa' Minhaaj Al-Sunnah.

Bloom, Jonathan M. in "The Introduction of Paper to the Islamic Lands and the Development of the Illustrated Manuscript", *Muqarnas*, XVII (2000): 22–23 (footnote 15) as quoted in http://www.islamic-awareness.org/Quran/Text/Mss/yem1f.html (accessed August 14, 2011)

"Codex Sana'a DAM 01-27.1 – A Qur'anic Manuscript from Mid-1st Century of Hijra" http://www.islamic-awareness.org/Quran/Text/Mss/soth.html (accessed August 14, 2011)

"Codex Sana'a DAM 01-29.2 – A Qur'anic Manuscript From 2nd Century of Hijra" http://www.islamic-awareness.org/Quran/Text/Mss/yem2a.html (accessed August 14, 2011)

Das, Sujit. "Ancient Qur'anic Manuscripts of Sana'a and Divine Downfall" http://www.faithfreedom.org/articles/quran-koran/ancient-qur%E2%80%99anic-manuscripts-of-sana%E2%80%99a-and-divine-downfall/ (accessed August 14, 2011)

Denffer, Ahmad von, 1994, *Ulum al-Qur'an*, Leicester, UK: Islamic Foundation

Dreibholz, Ursula. 1999, "Preserving a Treasure: the Sana'a Manuscripts." *Museum International: Islamic Collections*, LI, no 3 (July), 21–25.

Gilchrist, John. 1989, *Jam'al-Quran: The Codification of the Qur'an Text.* Mondeor, South Africa: MERCSA, http://www.answering-islam.org/Gilchrist/Jam/chap7.html (accessed, August 14, 2011)

Heger, Christoph, "A Qur'an Palimpsest from the Sanaa Qur'ans" http://www.christoph-heger.de/palimpse.htm (accessed August 14, 2011)

Lester, Toby. 1999, "What is the Koran?", *The Atlantic Monthly* (January). http://www.theatlantic.com/issues/99jan/koran.htm (accessed August 14, 2011)

Masood, Steven. 2001, *The Bible and the Qur'an: A Question of Integrity*, Cumbria, UK: OM Publishing.

"The Oldest Qur'anic Manuscripts" http://www.youtube.com/watch?v=iNdvsLh128Q (accessed August 14, 2011)

"Oldest Yemeni Quran differs from Uthman Quran today" http://www.youtube.com/watch?v=OLSEaPxePZc&playnext=1&list=PLBBB589C38BF5185E (accessed August 14, 2011)

"The Original Quran?" http://4freedoms.ning.com/group/argumentation/forum/topics/the-original quran?xg_source=activity (accessed August 14, 2011)

Puin, Gerd. 1999, Letter published by Christoph Heger, January https://groups.google.com/group/soc.religion.islam/browse_thread/thread/e5a6f19bb97e77cc/8e2774ca8e2e08bb?hl=de&lnk=gst&q=puin#8e2774ca8e2e08bb (accessed August 14, 2011)

------ 2002, "Observations on Early Qur'an Manuscripts in Sana'a." *In What the Koran Really Says: Language, Text and Commentary*, edited by Ibn Warraq, 739–744. Amherst, NY: Promethius Book.

Puin, Gerd as quoted in "The Oldest Qur'anic Manuscripts" http://www.youtube.com/watch?v=iNdvsLh128Q (accessed August 9, 2011)

Puin, Gerd, as quoted in "Oldest Yemeni Quran differs from Uthman Quran today" http://www.youtube.com/watch?v=OLSEaPxePZc&playnext=1&list=PLBBB589C38BF5185E (accessed August 9, 2011).

"The Qur'anic Manuscripts" http://www.islamic-awareness.org/Quran/Text/Mss/ (accessed August 14, 2011)

"Re: The Sanaa Manuscripts & the Koran" http://www.youtube.com/watch?v=hpwITk_ec7g (accessed August 14, 2011)

"Re: response to Re: The Sanaa Manuscripts & the Koran" [1/2] http://www.youtube.com/watch?v=Kb5OFJ6Ca8w (accessed August 14, 2011)

"Response to Re: The Sanaa Manuscripts & the Koran" http://www.youtube.com/watch?v=tqYyplzvgtc (accessed August 14, 2011)

"The Sana'a Manuscripts", http://www.unesco.org/webworld/mdm/visite/sanaa/en/present1.html (accessed August 14, 2011)

"Sana'a Manuscripts: Uncovering a Treasure of Words." UNESCO Courier, no. 5 (May 2007): 9.

Sookhdeo, Patrick as quoted in "The Oldest Qur'anic Manuscripts" http://www.youtube.com/watch?v=iNdvsLh128Q (accessed August 14, 2011)

Taher, Abul. 2000, "Querying the Koran: Orthodox Muslims believe that this ancient Islamic text is the unchanging Word of God. One Scholar is daring to question it." *The Guardian* (8 Aug). http://www.guardian.co.uk/education/2000/aug/08/highereducation.theguardian (accessed August 14, 2011)

Tzortzis, Hamza Andreas. "Dr. Puin and the Yemeni Manuscripts Taken from 'The Qur'an and the Orientalists' by Mohar Ali" http://hamzatzortzis.blogspot.com/2008/07/dr-puin-yemeni-manuscripts.html (accessed August 14, 2011)

von Bothmer, Hans-Casper Graf. 1987, "Masterworks of Islamic Book Art: Koranic Calligraphy and Illumination in the Manuscripts found in the Great Mosque in Sana'a" in *Yemen: 3000 Years of Art and Civilisation in Arabia Felix,* edited by Werner Dunn, 178–193. Innsbruck: Pinguin-Verlag

"Was there something wrong with early Qur'anic fragments/specimens found in the great mosque of Sanaa in Yemen?" http://www.answering-christianity.com/karim/mosque_of_sanaa.htm (accessed August 14, 2011)

Wild, Stefan, "Stefan Wild: The History of the Quran | Is the Quran the Word of God?" http://www.bible-quran.com/stefan-wild-history-quran/ (accessed August 14, 2011)

"Why the Quran is not from God: The Sana Manuscripts" http://www.youtube.com/watch?v=3JEQ4_qfyLI&feature=related (accessed August 14, 2011)

THE BIBLE, THE QUR'AN, AND THE SPACE IN BETWEEN:
Telling the Story[1]

Brent Neely[2]

What do we expect from a divinely-inspired book? To qualify as "revelation" must it answer all our questions? Must its language itself be somehow miraculous, almost super-human? Should it unveil the mysteries of modern science or be replete with uncannily accurate predictions? Must it inspire reverence from more people than any other book does? Who is to adjudicate these things?

In the contrast between the claims of Christian and Muslim faith there is probably no more fundamental arena of conflict than that of the "scriptures." In some sense, *all* contested issues (from the Trinity to the crucifixion to the political nature of religion) lead back to the texts that are marshalled to support one's contentions. In the encounter between Christian and Muslim books, the polemical comparison between the Bible and Qur'an is at times reduced to a contest over whose book is "best," truly "inerrant," or bears the surest marks of "inspiration".

Comparing Bible and Qur'an: The questions to ask

The "battle of the books" can easily become a frustrating exchange. Is "brass-knuckle" debate over the accuracy or flaws of either book the only option for us as believers? Might there be another angle for comparing the Christian and Muslim scriptures with their related but largely incommensurable messages?

---

[1] This article was first published in the CSIOF Bulletin, 2012, pp28–37.
[2] Brent Neely has served in the Middle East for some eighteen years in varying capacities, including being a Lecturer at the Nazareth Theological College.

The misdirection of much debate is partly due to the failure to consider prior questions like: *What is divine inspiration and what would it look like in a book anyhow? What about genre issues? What is the structure of faith; the character and purpose of God; the predicament of humanity; the nature of salvation?* Having very different views of God, humanity, and history, the two religions naturally have rather different expectations when it comes to the shape of en-scriptured revelation. There is, of course, an element of circularity to all this: our expectations are shaped by the books we already accept as inspired. Nonetheless, I want to argue for the value of approaches to the comparison of Bible and Qur'an that focus elsewhere than on questions of accuracy/error, miracles of language, and so on. In the rest of the essay we will hone in on the contrasting notions of Salvation History evidenced in the Bible and the Qur'an.

Bible and Qur'an: Their retrospective views

An examination of the salvation-historical perspectives of these books involves some sense of the books' relation to prior "books," perhaps that of the Qur'an to the Bible (or *tawrat, injil*, etc.) or that of the New Testament to the Old Testament (Hebrew Bible). We must note in passing that the Qur'an alleges some sort of distortion or corruption (*tahrif*) of the former Scriptures. However, for present purposes, it is crucial to understand that here we are examining the Qur'an's own *idealized view* of the history of revelation; we are interested in its own conception of its relation to, say, the supposed "original" *Torah* or Gospel. Dealing with the charge that the current Bible has been "corrupted" is for another occasion.

The Christian Story

A critical problem in relating Muslim scripture to the Bible is precisely this matter of the glaringly different conceptions of salvation history. There is a major divide between what the Christian and Muslim books tell us that God has always been up to in our world. The biblical pattern might be outlined this way: Creation → Fall → Covenant/Election → Exodus → Kingdom → Exile → Messianic Promise → Messianic Redemption → Final Conflict/Judgment → New Creation. The biblical sweep can be refracted through different prisms, such as God's sovereign reign, the unfolding of divine glory, the story of redemption, and so on. The principal point is that from a Christian view, the Bible is a story, a God-centred drama of the universe in which humanity participates and experiences both his judgment and salvation.

For the Christian, the Bible is a single, over-arching story with a beginning, middle, and end. God's promise to restore a radically sin-marred humanity is channelled through a man and nation (Abraham/Israel), but the chosen people too stand under judgment and in need of redemption. The story comes to a climax in an "end-time" intervention. According to prophetic promise, God himself acts in sacrificial love. God is unveiled in the shocking reversal of the death and resurrection of the messianic Son, Jesus of Nazareth. This establishes the restoration of the "overt" reign of God on his earth, the unseating of evil, the redemption of sinners, the start of a new creation—all to be confirmed and completed at the Second Coming.

For our purposes, three points about the Bible story need underlining:

1. The Grand Narrative of the Bible is progressive and developmental. Each stage strains forward to the next and is self-consciously incomplete, awaiting the looming climax. The stages of the story are not interchangeable and random in sequence. Abraham had to be called out, Israel had to emerge and be ransomed, Israel had to stumble in her vocation, etc., *and all in that order.* This necessary sequencing and a promise-fulfilment relationship is vital to the link between the Old and New Testaments, which have been likened to a seed (OT) which comes to full flower (NT).

2. The eschatological fulfilment represented by Jesus is the climactic, long-promised, yet surprising, fulfilment of ancient designs—designs built in to the beginning of the story. The Messiah comes as the realization of a prophetic promise. The new heavens and new earth are a resplendent, unprecedented reality, but they are still in continuity with what came before. The New Jerusalem of Revelation answers to the Eden of Genesis. God's good purposes for a world gone awry in the beginning are finally realized. A typological fulfilment pattern is a dominant hermeneutic in the New Testament's use of the Old (Testament).

3. In accomplishing the redemption and restoration of his world, Jesus comes in a long line of preceding leaders, messengers, and prophets, but he is far more than any of these. As "Son" and "Immanuel" he is not simply "the best in category" he is alone in his category.

The Muslim Story

In one sense, it is not possible to discuss the Qur'anic view of (holy) history without reference to the Bible because of the conscious, direct, or allusive reference in the Qur'an to the prior revelations and prophets. At least nominally, a large number of "biblical" characters are taken as divinely-sent messengers. Examples include Adam, Noah, Abraham, Joseph, Moses, David, Jonah, Jesus, and others. Now, the Bible clearly is not a simple tale, written by a single author at one sitting; it must be read carefully across time and genres as a meta-story. Having said that, the Qur'an's structure is even less a seamless narrative by comparison. It is neither chronological nor principally designed as a story. However, one *can* detect an implied structure of reality behind its exhortations, commands, and allusive tales. There is an *implied* story, a salvation history.

The gist is that, from the start, the only overwhelmingly sovereign Creator-God calls all humanity to submission, obedience, and recognition of his unvarying oneness. From the failing of Adam and Eve onwards, humanity's problem has been one of straying, weakness, and temptation towards idolatry—our deficiency being a failure to take "guidance," our need for divine law. Humankind is prone to thanklessness and forgetfulness towards God. So, God repeatedly, throughout history, sends revelation as a "reminder" (e.g., Q6:68–72; 10:71). Humanity's "salvation" does not consist in a restoration from radical sinfulness to intimacy with a personal God—his essence remains inscrutable in any case. It lies rather with submission to his revealed will and with a turning from all idolatry, all "association" of anything else with him.

According to the Qur'an, through the long trail of history, God's dealings with recalcitrant humanity have entailed warnings, punishments, and beckoning back to the "straight path" through a series of prophets, "biblical" and otherwise. God's gracious guidance orders humanity's relationship to God and minutely structures society. The divine summons is proclaimed in the Qur'an against a backdrop of the approaching final judgment. At the last cataclysm, all will be raised from death to horrific torment in the Fire or limitless pleasures in Paradise. So, between creation and judgment we have an impressive succession of messengers culminating in the dispensation of Muhammad, the greatest, the final prophet. His scope is universal, and he is also "eschatological," at least in the sense that he brings the *final* (imminent?) warning of the coming Day. No new prophet is to emerge after him.

Thus, the Islamic appeal, which is sometimes detailed as a call to believe in God, the prophets, the "books", angels, the last day, and so on (Q2:285; 4:136), may be boiled down to the charge to believe in "God and his messenger". The Messenger comes with a dire alert! The Day of Judgment thunders in the pages of the book, and each one awaits an awesome accounting based on some combination of works and the inscrutable will of God. For the blessed, the reward of Paradise awaits, for the damned, the Fire. The Qur'anic story may be one of prediction, promise and warning, reward and punishment, but it is not a biblical-style narrative pregnant with the themes of fulfilment and redemption.

Along with the Qur'anic conception of the human predicament and divine prescription comes a particular conception of the mission, role, and sequence of the former prophets and prior "books". In general, the Qur'anic references to the prior scriptures understand the revelation given to Muhammad as one of confirmation of that which God sent before. So, even the mission of Jesus was quite like that of Muhammad himself. Jesus brought the Gospel[3] as guidance (*huda*), light (*nur*), and confirmation (*musaddiq*) of the *Torah* before him (cf. Q5:46). The Qur'an may present Muhammad as the last prophet, but his dispensation is primarily a reiteration and renewal of God's guidance (e.g. Q2:136; 3:3, 48; 4:152; 9:111). Q4:163: "We inspired you as we inspired Noah and the prophets after." Essentially, the various revelations are the same (Q4:136). The relation of the Qur'an to the past is basically one of confirmation, repetition, and then supersession.

The Qur'an's use of the biblical base is terse and moralistic, apologetic, and provides a template for the prophet Muhammad

---

[3] Jesus is conceived of as a prophet bearing a revelation or a "book", the Gospel/*Injil*.

himself. The former messengers predicted his coming; brought the same message; faced the same opposition and vindication; and fit the pattern of Muhammad's own ministry. If the Qur'an and the Bible were conjoined organisms to be surgically separated, a clean division could be achieved with relative ease. If, on the other hand, we had the same goal of separating the Old and New Testaments, the operation would be far more hazardous and intricate. We might say the two share a comprehensive vascular system. The Qur'an's depiction of its religious role is one of purification and restoration, sequentially final, but not linked to former revelation in such a way that a continued appropriation of it is dynamically essential.[4]

It may be the case that salvation history climaxes with the prophet and the "criterion" of his book (cf. Q3:4), but it is hard to see his era as an *entirely new thing of a wholly different order*. There is no transposition to an altogether different key when we move from prior monotheisms to Islam as there is, for example, when we move from the dispensation of Moses to that of Jesus in the Gospel of John or the book of Hebrews. Though there are verses in the Qur'an assuming the prediction of Muhammad's mission in the former books (Q61:6; 7:157; 48:29), there is no extended engagement of biblical texts showing how the trials and aspirations of God's people have been resolved with the sending of the Qur'an and its messenger. We have no typological fulfilment of the scriptures "in these last days," a realisation, as the hymn would have it, of "the hopes and fears of all the years."

Certainly, for the Muslim, the prophet brought a life-example and revelation like no other, banishing the age of "ignorance" (*jahiliya*). Nonetheless, he at most represents the paradigm of "prophet" taken to the ultimate degree. Muhammad may be the "best and the last" in a succession of divine restorations, but, still, he does not represent a fundamentally distinct type of intervention by God in the order of Jesus the Son.

And what of the prophetic traditions (Hadiths) which so often interpret the Qur'an for the Muslim? A famous tradition holds that all the "prophets are brothers." Muhammad comes in as

---

[4] See J.D. McAuliffe's article in J. C. Reeves (ed.), *Bible and Qur'an: Essays in Scriptural Intertextuality*, Society of Biblical Literature, 2003, pp108–110.

something of a first among equals.[5] Very interesting is the comparison between Muhammad and Moses in the famous tradition in which, *at the resurrection, it will be unclear whether Muhammad or Moses first regains consciousness from the "cosmic swoon" before the rest of creation* (Bukhari 9.83.52).[6] Other Hadiths tell us that Muhammad received six privileges unique to him among the prophets[7] or that he is like the final brick completing a splendid house (symbolizing the entirety of the prophets) (Bukhari 4.56.734). The versions of the story of Muhammad's Ascent to Heaven likewise see the prophets as quite interchangeable, only with Muhammad coming in emphatically as the final one. The point is that even when the texts magnify the person of Muhammad over other prophets, we are still dealing with a difference of degree, not of kind.

Setting the two "revelations" side by side once again, the point is often made, but worth restating: In Islam, God's highest revelation to humanity is a book. In the Christian faith, it is a person, the Word made flesh. Both our books purport to bring "Good News," but their essences are in striking contrast. At its core, the Qur'an is an announcement (of promise and threat) from God, a command or "law," if you will. At its heart, the Bible is a story of what a loving God has done for us in Christ.

Tell the story[8]

When it comes to witness across the religious and cultural divide, what might be the practical implications *related to the Christian–Muslim disjunction we have been describing*? Speaking from within the Christian fold, one option might be to look for ways to adapt or contextualize any presentation of our faith in line with Muslim expectation. However, the disjunction in salvation-historical schemes is hardly a peripheral or cosmetic matter. We are dealing with the very shape of reality and the metanarrative of what God is about in the world. Adjust too much and it is no longer the Christian faith that is being communicated!

---

[5] Later popular and mystical legends super-exalting Muhammad are another matter.
[6] *Sahih Bukhari*, online at http://www.cmje.org/religious-texts/hadith/bukhari/ (accessed 5 September 2012).
[7] See, for example, standard commentaries on Q33:40.
[8] I am thankful here for my access to an unpublished essay by Scott Bridger on *The Christian Use of the Qur'an*.

Another possible response to the dilemma of the contrasting scriptures is one we have already mentioned. That is, of course, the intense apologetic effort to demonstrate the factual truth and miraculous nature of the Bible over against the Qur'an. This kind of endeavour is fraught with challenges and can elicit unintended consequences, but a few hardy debaters may well thrive in this fray.

I want to forward another suggestion which is neither "accommodationist" nor combatively polemical. Put very simply: "tell the story". As has been intimated, the Qur'an is a message, a summons, an eschatological warning, etc. But, for the most part, it is not a story. Narratives do appear in its pages, of course, but mainly in sequences alluding to the prophets. These allusive references throughout the text point to the *implied* "story" of Islamic salvation history discussed above. The Christian Bible, on the other hand, not only is full of stories, but is best read as an entire story—the record of God's action in his world. It is, in fact, *the* story, His Story. So, for reasons spiritual, dogmatic, and structural it is no wonder that the biblical climax, the story of Christ crucified (and risen), is not what a Muslim is programmed to expect in the *injil*. But, we can also say, with great wonder and thanks, many Muslims *do* find that this story, this "foolishness," becomes for them the power and wisdom and redemption of God (1 Cor 1:18-25)!

The Bible is the story around which our lives, all lives, Muslim lives, are meant to be oriented. It is the story of human need, divine grace, and the drama of salvation. It is the story we so need—God's own glorious, cosmic story. The wonder of redemption is that the Lord invites us to join him in it. The Christian hope and plea is not so much to win a battle with the Muslim over the quality of one's book; it is that many from all backgrounds might encounter Christ in the pages of the Bible and find that with him are "the words of life." May the Spirit empower the telling of the story so that many may see the light of God's own glory shining in the face of Jesus (2 Cor 4:6).

Bibliography

Bridger, J. Scott, *Christian Exegesis of the Qur'an: A Critical Analysis of the Apologetic Use of the Qur'an in Select Medieval and*

Contemporary Arabic Texts, Eugene, Oregon: Pickwick Publications, 2015.

Donner, Fred, *Narratives of Islamic Origins*, SLAEI 14, Princeton: Darwin Press, 1998.

Guillaume, A., trans., *The Life of Muhammad: A Translation of Ibn Ishaq's Sirat Rasul Allah*, Karachi: Oxford University Press, 2001.

McAuliffe, Jane Dammen, "The Prediction and Prefiguration of Muhammad," in *Bible and Qur'an: Essays in Scriptural Intertextuality* (John C. Reeves, editor), Society of Biblical Literature, 2003, 107-132.

-------- *Qur'anic Christians, An Analysis of Classical and Modern Exegesis*, Cambridge: Cambridge University Press, 1991.

Sahih Bukhari: Online at http://www.cmje.org/religious-texts/hadith/bukhari/ (accessed 5 September 2012).

COMMENTARIES ON THE QUR'AN:
Views of Biblical Characters and Christians

Peter Riddell[1]

For Christians who are interested in studying Islam and engaging with Muslims, an understanding of the structure and teachings of the Qur'an is of the utmost importance, particularly those teachings about themes common to Christianity and Islam. It is equally important that such students of the Qur'an do not see the text as existing within a vacuum.

While some verses of the Qur'an may appear straightforward in meaning, others are not so clear. The Qur'an, as Islam's most sacred text, needs to be interpreted in order to play a role as the key guiding text for Muslims. The field of interpretation, or exegesis, is as important to the study of the Qur'an as it is in the study of the Bible.

Surrounding the Qur'an is a vast collection of literature that can help with understanding the teachings of Islam's sacred text. The Christian student of the Qur'an needs to be also familiar to some extent with this body of literature. Such a familiarity will provide greater depth of understanding but it will also avoid superficial and sometimes misleading readings of the Qur'anic text.

Muslims have interpreted the message of the Qur'an since the time of Muhammad, messenger of Islam. In the early centuries of Islamic history, Muslim scholars had vigorous, and sometimes bitter, debates about how to interpret the Qur'anic text. These early commentators were extremely cautious; they took care to avoid adding their own perspectives in understanding the sacred text of

---

[1] Dr Peter Riddell serves as Vice Principal Academic and Senior Research Fellow in Islam at the Melbourne School of Theology. He has published extensively on Islam and Christian–Muslim Relations, with Qur'anic exegesis being one of his fields of specialisation.

Islam. They also regarded some questions as being inappropriate; any suggestions of Qur'anic textual error, incompleteness, or borrowing from non-Islamic sources were not considered acceptable in these early centuries. So, on the one hand, Muslims needed to understand and explain their sacred book; on the other hand, they felt very constrained in doing so.

It is recorded that Muhammad's colleagues, known as the Companions, commented on the meanings of the verses of the Qur'an. This earliest commentary activity was helped by the canonisation of the hadith collections, which include many volumes purporting to record Muhammad's statements and deeds. This was vitally important in setting guidelines for early Qur'anic commentary activity. A hadith report from the collection of al-Tirmidhi stated, "Whoever interprets the Qur'an according to his own light will go to Hell."[2] This was interpreted to signal that all commentary on the Qur'an should be consistent with the recorded statements and deeds of Muhammad. In this way, Muhammad's role as ideal model for Muslims was consolidated.

The following example demonstrates how the Hadith reports could add to the meaning of the Qur'an. We have three Qur'anic verses taken from *Sura* 38 that refer to David, a great King of ancient Israel who is regarded as a prophet in Islam:

> [Q38:17] *Have patience at what they say, and remember Our Servant David, the man of strength: for he ever turned (to Allah).*
> [18] *It was We that made the hills declare, in unison with him, Our Praises, at eventide and at break of day,*
> [19] *And the birds gathered (in assemblies): all with him did turn (to Allah).*
> [20] *We strengthened his kingdom, and gave him wisdom and sound judgment in speech and decision.*[3]

If we follow the early rule that explaining the Qur'an should be done by reference to the Hadith, we then turn to the Hadith collections to see what they have to say about David. There are hundreds of reports available across the collections, including the following:

---

[2] A.J. Wensinck, *A Handbook of Early Muhammadan Tradition*, Leiden: Brill,1971, p131.
[3] *The Qur'an,* translated by Yusuf Ali, 2001 Goodword Books, New Delhi

> *Sahih Al-Bukhari, Volume 2, Book 21, Number 231*:
> Narrated Abdullah bin 'Amr bin Al-'As: Allah's Apostle told me, *The most beloved prayer to Allah is that of David and the most beloved fasts to Allah are those of David. He used to sleep for half of the night and then pray for one third of the night and again sleep for its sixth part and used to fast on alternate days.*
>
> *Sahih Muslim, Book 004, Number 1734*:
> Buraida reported on the authority of his father that the Messenger of Allah (may peace be upon him) had said: *'Abdullah b. Qais or al-Ash'ari has been gifted with a sweet melodious voice out of the voices of the family of David.*
>
> *Sahih Al-Bukhari, Volume 3, Book 34, Number 286*:
> Narrated Al-Miqdam: The Prophet said, *Nobody has ever eaten a better meal than that which one has earned by working with one's own hands. The Prophet of Allah, David used to eat from the earnings of his manual labour.*

We see that in addition to the Qur'anic references to David praising God together with flocks of birds, and to him being wise "in speech and decision" the Hadith reports provide additional detail: he interspersed sleep and prayer during his nights; he was the forerunner of a line of beautiful singers; he used to buy food "from the earnings of his manual labour".

The Early Commentaries

As commentary activity on the Qur'an developed across subsequent centuries, debates emerged about style and method. Some commentators, who represented the early mainstream, favoured a very literalist approach to explaining Qur'anic verses as they prepared independent commentaries. They mainly drew on exegetical Hadith reports, linking them with the Qur'anic verses in question. This approach to exegesis was known as *tafsir bi'l-ma'thur*, or "interpretation based upon transmitted sources".[4]

Against this approach was that favoured by more philosophically-minded commentators. They developed more rationalist methods of commentary writing, known as *tafsir bi'l-ra'y*, or "interpretation based on individual reasoning" although this

---

[4] Jane Dammen McAuliffe, *The Cambridge Companion to the Qur'ān*, Cambridge, Cambridge, 2006, p189.

approach to Qur'anic exegesis had to wait until the 12th century for its greatest exponents to appear.

The Hadith-based approach of *tafsir bi'l-ma'thur* dominated the commentary writing in the first three centuries after the death of Muhammad in 632. A very early commentator to draw on this approach in producing an independent commentary was **Muqatil ibn Sulayman** (d. 765). We can see his style in his commentary on verse 7 of the opening *Sura al-Fatiha*. In the preceding verse, God is implored to give guidance to the "Straight Way" Verse 7 of the Qur'an then defines this Straight Way with a contrasting statement:

> [Q1:7] *The Way of those on whom You have bestowed Your Grace, not of those who earned Your Anger, nor of those who went astray.*

How is Muqatil, a very early pioneer of Qur'anic commentary, to explain this enigmatic verse? He chooses an uncontroversial path in terms of methodology: he gives his interpretation and then cites Hadith reports in support. Unfortunately for Jews and Christians, his interpretation casts them in a very unfavourable light:

> [Muqatil]: *The path of those whom You have blessed:* that is, We have indicated the way of those who We have blessed, that is, the proofs of those whom God has blessed with prophethood ...
>
> *Not those against whom You have sent Your wrath*: that is, a religion other than the Jewish one, against which God was wrathful. Monkeys and pigs were made from them.
>
> *Nor those who are astray*: God is saying: "And not the religion of the polytheists," that is, the Christians.[5]

Muqatil then offers four Hadith reports to support his interpretation of these verses. Although the chosen Hadith reports do not themselves identify Jews and Christians by name, the fact that Muqatil turns to the Hadith points to the centrality of this method of interpretation in these early years of Islam's history.

The most important name in setting the foundations for commentary writing on the Qur'an in early Islam is that of Abu

---

[5] A. Rippin & J. Knappert (eds.) *Textual Sources for the Study of Islam*, Chicago: University of Chicago, 1986, p46.

Ja'far Muhammad ibn Jarir **al-Tabari** (d. 310/923). He followed the methodology of *tafsir bi'l-ma'thur* in writing his multi-volume commentary entitled *Jami` al-bayan `an tafsir al-qur'an* [Collection of Explanations for the Interpretation of the Qur'an]. He favoured literal interpretations of Qur'anic words and phrases, pointing to and reinforcing popular engagement with the Qur'an by the Muslim community in his time.

As with Muqatil, the commentary of al-Tabari includes some material that is unfavourable for Jews and Christians. His approach to interpreting Q6:115, a verse that touches on the thorny question of some communities having changed the revelation they received from God, is to affirm a literal understanding of the verse, adding clarification of the culprits for the benefit of his reader.

> [Q6:115] *And the Word of your Lord has been fulfilled in truth and in justice. None can change His Words. And He is the All-Hearer, the All-Knower.*

> [Al-Tabari]: The word of God meant in this verse is the Quran. This word is complete in truth and justice. Nothing can change Allah's word which he revealed in his books. The liars cannot add or delete from Allah's books. This is referring without a doubt to the Jews and Christians because they are the people of the books which were revealed to their prophets. Allah is revealing that the words they (the people of the book) are corrupting were not revealed by Allah, but Allah's word cannot be changed or substituted.[6]

Another commentator who adopted a similar approach was Abu Ishaq Ahmad b. Ibrahim **al-Tha`labi** al-Nisaburi (d. 427/1035). His commentary, *al-Kashf wa al-bayan `an tafsir al-Qur'an* [Unveiling and Clarifying the Interpretation of the Qur'an], mixed hadith accounts with lengthy narratives, pointing to the important role of story as a teaching device in the early history of Islam.

Several later commentators adopted his method, including `Ala al-Din Abu al-Hasan `Ali b. Muhammad Ibrahim `Umar (d. 1340), better known as **al-Khazin** (the treasurer, storer). His commentary, entitled *Lubab al-ta'wil fi ma`ani al-tanzil* [The Core of

---

[6] S. Shamoun, "Al-Tabari's Notes on the Veracity of the Bible", http://www.answering-islam.org/Quran/Bible/tabari_tafsir.htm, accessed 5 August 2017.

Interpretation in the Meanings of Revelation], carries a rich vein of narrative throughout, as seen below in the commentary on Q18:9–10, verses that address the Story of the Seven Sleepers of Ephesus, a popular legend in early Christianity:[7]

> [Q18:9] *Do you think that the people of the Cave and the Inscription were a wonder among Our signs?*
>
> [10] *When the young men fled for refuge to the Cave, they said: "Our Lord Bestow on us mercy from Yourself, and facilitate for us our affair in the right way!"*

Al-Khazin draws on the early Islamic biographers Muhammad b. Ishaq and Muhammad b. Yasar for a lengthy story, from which we provide the following short excerpt:

> [Al-Khazin]: There was confusion among the Christians; their sins were great, and their kings oppressed them to the point of worshipping idols and offering up sacrifices to them. Nevertheless, a remnant preserved the religion of Christ, continuing to worship God and his Oneness. Among the kings who did [abandon the faith] was a certain king of Rome named Daqyanus; he worshipped idols, offered sacrifices to them and killed any who refused to comply. He would descend upon villages of [the] Rom[an empire], and he would not leave anybody in these villages who did not abandon their faith to worship idols; those who refused were killed. When he descended upon the village of the Friends of the Cave, which was named Ephesus, the faithful hid from him and fled wherever they could. So he gathered a group of pagans and ordered them to follow them. This group followed the faithful to their [hiding] places, and brought them before Daqyanus, who made them choose between death and worshipping idols. Some preferred life, while others refused to worship any but the One God, and they were killed. When the strong in faith saw this, they gave themselves up for punishment and death; they were killed, cut up into pieces, and their remains were left on the walls and by the gates of the city. With the agitation was at its greatest, and seeing that, the young people gathered a great quantity of provisions; they prayed, fasted, gave alms, and extolled God's name. They were of the aristocracy of Rome and were eight in number. They wept and called upon Almighty God, saying: "Our God is the Lord

---

[7] "The Seven Sleepers of Ephesus", http://www.newadvent.org/cathen/05496a.htm, accessed 5 August 2017.

of the Heavens and the Earth. We will never call on any but Him, for such would be an infringement. Remove this temptation from Your faithful servants."[8]

In this narrative, al-Khazin has proposed that some Christians strayed from the truth, while some Christians remained faithful to the One God. This reinforced the growing perception among Muslims that Christianity, once a true revelation, had become corrupted.

Philosophical Commentaries: *tafsir bi'l-ra'y*

In time, the field of Qur'anic exegesis became increasingly open to more philosophical questions, moving beyond use of hadith and narrative to consider issues raised by some of the great debates such as that between the Mu`tazilites[9] and the *ahl al-Hadith* (literalists) which related to question such as the justice of God and human free will. The result was a series of voluminous commentaries, such as those produced by Abu al-Qasim Jar Allah Mahmud ibn `Umar **al-Zamakhshari** (d. 538/1144) and Muhammad b. `Umar Fakhr al-Din **al-Razi** (d. 1210).

Al-Zamakhshari's monumental work, *al-Kashshaf `an haqa'iq ghawamid al-tanzil wa-`uyun al-aqawil fi wujuh al-ta'wil* [The Unveiler of the Real Meanings of the Hidden Matters of What Was Sent Down and the Choicest Statements About the Various Aspects of its Interpretation] does what its title suggests: it moves beyond surface discussion of stories to seek "hidden" meanings. Al-Zamakhshari was a Mu'tazilite, embracing a set of views that were no longer mainstream during his lifetime. This caused his commentary to be somewhat controversial, though the sheer force of his rigorous scholarship ensured that the work would continue to be used by subsequent scholars.

On the question of the authenticity of the Christian Scriptures, al-Zamakhshari maintained an orthodox Muslim view, as seen in the following excerpt of his commentary on Q4:169 which, though demonstrating his exegetical method of using reasoning, is clearly rejectionist:

---

[8] Khazin, A. a. `Ali al-, *Lubab al- Ta'wil fi Ma`ani al-Tanzil*, Beirut: Dar al-Thaqafa, n.d., vol. 3, pp186–87. Trans. P. Riddell.

[9] The Mu'tazila (Mu'tazilites) were rationalist theologians who emerged in the 8th century and who argued for views such as free will and the necessary justice of God.

[Q4:169] *Except the path of Hell; they will abide therein forever. And that, for Allah, is [always] easy.*

[Al-Zamakhshari]: The story received among Christians is that God is one in essence and three persons, (*akanim*) the person of the Father, the person of the Son and the person of the Holy Spirit. And they verily mean by the person of the Father, the Being, and by the person of the Son, knowledge, and by the person of the Holy Spirit, life. And this supposes that God is the third of three, or, if not, that there are three gods. And that which the Koran here refers to is the clear statement of theirs, that God and Christ and Mary are three gods and that the Christ is a child (*walad*) of God from Mary.[10]

Fakhr al-Din al-Razi, born just after the death of al-Zamakhshari, drew heavily on the latter's commentary in his own *Mafatih al-ghaib* [Keys to the Hidden], though he carefully avoided the Mu'tazili elements of his exegetical predecessor. Running to thirty volumes, al-Razi's work has been accused of being overly verbose. His detailed style is seen in the following excerpt that records various Muslim interpretations of the end of Jesus' time on earth, discussing the enigmatic term *mutawaffika* used in Q3:55.[11] Al-Razi states of the following diverse interpretations, "these are the total said views of those who interpreted the verse according to the literal meaning"[12]:

[Q3:55] *Lo! God said: "O Jesus! Verily, I shall cause thee to die [mutawaffika], and shall exalt thee unto Me, and cleanse thee of [the presence of] those who are bent on denying the truth; and I shall place those who follow thee [far] above those who are bent on denying the truth, unto the Day of Resurrection. In the end, unto Me you all must return, and I shall judge between you with regard to all on which you were wont to differ.*

---

[10] S. Zwemer, *The Moslem Doctrine of God*, New York: American Tract Society, 1905, 80–81, citing vol. I. of the *Kashshaf*, p241.
[11] Translated by various modern scholars as "cause thee to die" (Asad), "recall you (from your mission)" (Malik), "gathering thee" (Pickthall), "take thee" (Yusuf Ali). http://www.alim.org/library/quran/ayah/compare/3/55/allah's-promise-to-isa-(jesus), accessed 10 August 2017.
[12] *Razi's al-Tafsir al-Kabir*, vol. 8, p. 74, cited in Faris al-Qayrawani, *Was Christ Really Crucified?*, Villach, Austria: Light of Life, 1994, pp59–62.

[Al-Razi]: *Cause you to die:* this is a statement made on the authority of Ibn Abbas, the expositor of the Quran, and Muhammad b. Ishaq. They said that the purpose was not to let his enemies, the Jews, to kill him. Then after that (God) honored Him (Jesus) by raising Him up to heaven. From this point on, Muslim scholars differed in three ways: a) Wahb [ibn Munabbih] said: He died for three hours, then was raised up; b) Muhammad b. Ishaq said: He died seven hours then God quickened Him and raised him up; c) al-Rabi b. Anas said: God caused Him to die when He raised Him up to heaven; for God said (in the Quran): "God takes the soul at the time of their death, and that which has not died, in its sleep." [13]

The waw ("and") regulates the word order: Since Jesus is alive, that means that God raised Him up to heaven first; then He will descend to kill the anti-Christ. After that God will cause Him to die.

The spiritual interpretation: this is the opinion of Abu Bakr al-Wasity: "(I cause you to die) of your lusts and the desires of your soul. Then He said: 'I raise you up to Me' because unless He dies to what is not but God He would never reach the knowledge of God. Also, when Jesus was raised up to heaven, He became like the angels: free of lusts, anger and reprehensible dispositions."

The complete ascension: that is Jesus, son of Mary, was raised up whole in both body and spirit, not only in spirit as some may think. What supports this interpretation is God's saying: "They would not cause You any harm."

I make you as if you died: Raising Jesus up to heaven, the eradication of any physical trace of Him from this earth, and the obliteration of His reports would make Him as if He really died. "Applying the name of one thing to another if they share similar properties and qualities, is permissible."
...

Compensation for the work: that is, God "has announced to Him the glad tidings of accepting His obedience and His deed. He revealed to Him (Jesus) the troubles and the toils He would suffer from His enemies as He spread His (God's) religion and law. He (God) would not forfeit His compensation or waste His reward."

---

[13] Al-Zumar 39:44

Prominent later exegetes of the *tafsir bi'l-ra'y* stream were 'Abd Allah ibn 'Umar ibn Muhammad ibn 'Ali Abu al-Khayr Nasir al-Din **al-Baydawi** (d. 1286) and Abdullah bin Ahmad bin Mahmud **al-Nasafi** (d. 710/1310). Al-Baydawi's concise two-volume commentary, *Anwar al-tanzil wa asrar al-ta'wil* [The Lights of Revelation and the Secrets of Interpretation] drew on diverse sources, but especially the commentary by al-Zamakhshari. It has received wide circulation throughout the Muslim world and is still commonly found in Muslim theological training institutions as part of the curriculum in *tafsir* studies. Al-Baydawi's commentary on topics relating to Christians and Christianity reflects orthodox viewpoints, as seen in the exegesis of Q5:51:

> [Q5:51]: *O you who have believed, do not take the Jews and the Christians as allies. They are [in fact] allies of one another. And whoever is an ally to them among you - then indeed, he is [one] of them. Indeed, Allah guides not the wrongdoing people.*
>
> [Al-Baydawi]: *O you who believe! Do not take the Jews and Christians as allies.* Do not rely on them and do not associate with them as close associates. *They are allies of each other.* ... And truly they agree on your separation from each of them, because of their union in faith and their consensus in opposing you. *And whoever from among you takes them as allies is one of them,* and whoever allies with them from among you is one of their number. This emphasis on the obligation to avoid them is as the Prophet (PBUH) said: "Their fire should not be seen", because their friends were hypocrites. *Allah does not guide the wrongdoers,* those who wronged themselves by allying with the unbelievers, or believers who ally with their enemies.[14]

Social Chaos and Exegetical Conservatism

For Sunni exegesis, al-Razi's commentary heralded the gradual closing of an era. The century of his death was marked by great upheaval in the Muslim heartlands, marked most significantly by the fall of Baghdad to the genocidal Mongols in 1258. The resulting social disarray provided the context for the emergence of two scholars, **Ibn Taymiyya** (d. 1328) and his student **Ibn Kathir**

---

[14] Nasir al-Din Abi Sa'id Abd Allah Abi Umar ibn Muhammad Al-Shirazi al-Baydawi, *Tafsir al-Baydawi al-musamma Anwar al-Tanzil wa Asrar al-Ta'wil*, Beirut: Dar al-Fikr, 1996, vol. 2, pp333–34. Trans. P. Riddell.

(d. 1373), whose approach to Qur'anic interpretation was to affirm a more literalist understanding of the surface meaning of the text. Ibn Kathir's *Tafsir al-Qur'an al-`azim* [Commentary on the Great Qur'an] has had a profound influence down the centuries. His call for a more structured exegesis prioritising Qur'an on Qur'an and supplementary use of Hadith and writings by the Companions appealed especially to more fundamentalist streams of Islamic thinking.

Jews and Christians do not fare well in Ibn Kathir's commentary on the Qur'an. For example, in the fighting verses in *Sura* 9 where the Qur'an calls for action against idolators and disbelievers, Ibn Kathir does not mince his works. An excerpt of his lengthy commentary is as follows:

> [Q9:30] *The Jews say, "Ezra is the son of Allah"; and the Christians say, "The Messiah is the son of Allah." That is their statement from their mouths; they imitate the saying of those who disbelieved [before them]. May Allah destroy them; how are they deluded?*
>
> [Ibn Kathir]: Allah the Exalted encourages the believers to fight the polytheists, disbelieving Jews and Christians, who uttered this terrible statement and utter lies against Allah, the Exalted. As for the Jews, they claimed that `Uzayr [Ezra] was the son of God, Allah is free of what they attribute to Him. As for the misguidance of Christians over `Isa, it is obvious. This is why Allah declared both groups to be liars,
>
> (*That is their saying with their mouths*), but they have no proof that supports their claim, other than lies and fabrications,
>
> (*resembling*), imitating,
>
> (*the saying of those who disbelieved aforetime.*) They imitate the previous nations who fell into misguidance just as Jews and Christians did,
>
> (*may Allah fight them*), Ibn `Abbas said, "May Allah curse them."

(*how they are deluded away from the truth*!) how they deviate from truth, when it is apparent, exchanging it for misguidance.[15]

A discussion of classical commentary writing on the Qur'an would not be complete without mention of Jalal al-Din al-Misri **al-Suyuti** al-Shafi'i (d. 911/1505). He was a prolific author, with one of his most famous works being the *Jalalayn* commentary, jointly authored with his teacher, Jalal al-Din **al-Mahalli** (d. 1459). This work, which has appeared in many editions and translations into other languages, is arguably the most widely distributed Qur'anic commentary throughout the history of Islam. In style, it provides a smorgasbord of exegetical material— hadith, narrative, linguistic discussion, philosophical reflection, variant readings and much more—but all at a relatively introductory level. The commentary avoids the kinds of controversial elements that caused so many other works to encounter major obstacles. Usually appearing in a single volume, the *Jalalayn* commentary is readily available in English translation thanks to the work of the Royal Aal al-Bayt Institute for Islamic Thought in Amman, Jordan. Its rendering into English ensures that this commentary will continue to exert significant influence among students of Islamic Studies, both Muslim and non-Muslim.

The *Jalalayn* commentary's offering on Q2:62 shows clearly the method of this commentary to present stand-alone comment covering various angles on the text, including linguistic information, but not entering into too much detail:

> [Q2:62]: *Indeed, those who believed and those who were Jews or Christians or Sabeans [before Prophet Muhammad]—those [among them] who believed in Allah and the Last Day and did righteousness—will have their reward with their Lord, and no fear will there be concerning them, nor will they grieve.*
>
> [Jalalayn]: Surely *those who believe* who believed before in the prophets (*and*) those of Jewry *(the Jews and the Christians and the Sabaeans)* a Christian or Jewish sect (*whoever*) from among them (*believes in God and the Last Day*) in the time of our Prophet (*and performs righteous deeds*) according to the Law given to him—(*their wage*) that is the reward for their

---

[15] http://www.qtafsir.com/index.php?option=com_content&task=view&id=2565, accessed 9 August 2017.

deeds (*is with their Lord and no fear shall befall them neither shall they grieve*). The singular person of the verbs *āmana* "believes" and *'amila* "performs" takes account of the singular form of man "whoever" but in what comes afterwards of the plural pronouns its plural meaning is taken into account.[16]

Exegesis beyond the Arab World: Southeast Asia

In the far-flung corners of the Muslim world, scholars writing in other languages referred directly to the great early Arabic commentaries. In the Malay world, `Abd al-Ra'uf b. Ali al-Fansuri al-Singkili (d. 1693) wrote *Tarjuman al-Mustafid* [The Interpreter of that which gives Benefit], using as its primary sources the commentaries of the Jalalayn, al-Baydawi and al-Khazin. Its readers were thus provided with a snapshot of various exegetical approaches: hadith-based, rationalist, and narrative.

In the following comment on Q19:30–37, `Abd al-Ra'uf follows the Jalalayn commentary closely in commenting on the verses which report Jesus speaking from the cradle. The message is orthodox in rejecting the Christian belief in the divinity of Jesus:[17]

> [`Abd al-Ra'uf]: 30. The child (*said: "Truly I am a servant of God. He has given me the Book*) of the Gospel (*and has made me a Prophet*).
>
> 31. (*"And He has made me of service*) to all mankind (*wherever I am, and has enjoined on me prayer and*) the giving of (alms as long as I *live*),
>
> 32. (*"and also to be devoted to my mother. He has not made me arrogant or disobedient*) to my Lord.
>
> 33. (*"And peace*) from God (*was on me the day I was born and will be on me the day I die and the day I am to be resurrected*)."
>
> 34. God declared: (*Such*) is the word telling that (*Jesus is the son of Mary. This is a true statement concerning which there is confusion*) among the Christians.

---

[16] Jalal al-Din al-Mahalli and Jalal al-Din al-Suyuti, *Tafsir al-Jalalayn*, trans. F. Hamza, Amman: Royal Aal al-Bayt Institute for Islamic Thought, 2007, p11.
[17] P. Riddell, *Transferring a Tradition*, Berkeley: Centers for South and Southeast Asian Studies, University of California, 1990, pp192–93.

35. (*God has not taken a son. He far transcends*) such things. (*When He wishes to create something, then He says: "Be", and it is.*) Among these things is the creation of Jesus without a father.

...

36. (*And*) declare: (*Truly God is my Lord and your Lord, so serve Him.*) What is stated here is (*the right path*) which leads to Heaven.

37. (*The sects*) of Christians (*quarrel among themselves*) in saying that either Jesus is the son of God, or a God beside Him, or a third member of a Trinity. (*Great will be the punishment for these unbelievers when they are present on the Day of Resurrection with all its uproar.*)

Modern Exegetes

With the colonisation of many Muslim societies by European powers in the 19th and 20th centuries, Qur'anic commentators were sure to respond, and in the 20th century there were some dynamic new developments in Qur'anic exegesis. These modern exegetes were fully conversant with the methods of their classical predecessors. However, a rapidly changing world called for new approaches and answers to the modern world's challenges.

The *Tafsir al-Manar* [The Lighthouse Commentary], a significant exegetical work from the 20th century, represents the joint output of Muhammad `**Abduh** (d. 1905) and Rashid **Rida** (d. 1935). The former served as Grand Mufti of Egypt from 1899–1905, and his lectures at al-Azhar University during this period provide the basis for the first part of this commentary, supplemented by the writings of his student Rida. In this work the two scholars sought to bridge the Qur'an and modern science, pointing out that Islamic thinking should be dynamic, not static, moving from medieval jurisprudence to address the issues of the modern age. This powerful message resonated throughout the Muslim world.

The *Tafsir al-Manar* inspired many commentaries in other Muslim languages, such as the commentary by the Indonesian scholar **Hamka** (d. 1981). Following its independence from Dutch colonial rule in 1945, Indonesia provided fertile ground for the revival of the more philosophical method of *tafsir bi'l-ra'y* in the late 20th and early 21st centuries. Hamka was influenced by Sufi thinking throughout his life, and his commentary, *Tafsir al-Azhar*, distils a rich collection of both classical and modern exegetical sources from the Arab world.

In his commentary on Q18:29, Hamka shows an open-mindedness on the question of human free will that is reminiscent of the earlier Mu'tazila:

> [18:29] *And say, "The truth is from your Lord, so whoever wills—let him believe; and whoever wills—let him disbelieve."* ...
>
> [Hamka]: The meaning is that truth comes from God, not from me and not from you. Truth is above us all. In confronting the truth, there is no difference between rich and poor people, or between strong or weak people. *Because of that, whoever so wishes can be strong in faith.* If one feels that truth is truly important, convinced within one's own heart, if one wishes one will be strong in faith. *And whoever so wishes, then he will abandon faith!* Because you are each given intellectual capacity. You yourself can consider and adhere to the truth. If you are strong in faith, you will save yourself, because you have followed the voice of your own intellect. And if you wish to abandon faith, then the one who will bear the consequences of this apostasy is none other than you.[18]

Nevertheless, more narrow and literalist approaches to Qur'anic exegesis also found a ready audience among 20th century Muslims. More assertive, and even angry, messages affirming black-and-white dichotomies among believers and non-believers were to be found in the multi-volume commentary by the Egyptian **Sayyid** Qutb (d. 1966). His *Fi zilal al-Qur'an* [In the Shade of the Qur'an], together with his other writings, inspired legions of political Islamist activists throughout the Muslim world and in the West.

The urgent activism of Sayyid Qutb is captured well in the following excerpt from his commentary on Q25:52:

> [Q25:52]: *So do not obey the disbelievers, and strive against them with the Qur'an a great striving.*
>
> [Sayyid Qutb] <u>Jihad by Means of The Qur'an</u> ...

---

[18] Hamka, *Tafsir Al-Azhar Juzu'15*, Jakarta: PT Pustaka Panjimas, 1982, pp198–99. Trans. P. Riddell.

"Had We so willed, We could have sent a warner to every city." (Verse 51) Such a course would have divided the task and made it easier to carry out. God, however, chose one of His servants, the last of His Messengers, and required him to address all mankind, so as to give them the same message which remains free from local variations. God also gave His messenger the Qur'an, so as to make it the address he drove home to them: *"Do not obey the unbelievers, but strive vigorously against them with this Qur'an."* (verse 52)

This Qur'an has great power and influence. It is irresistible. When God's Messenger addressed the Arabs with it, it shook their hearts and consciences. They tried hard to counter its effects, employing every means at their disposal, but all their efforts were useless. The Quraysh elders used to say to their people: *"Do not listen to this Qur'an, but rather [speak] frivolously about it, so that you might gain the upper hand."* (Q41:26) This betrayed their profound fear that the Qur'an would touch their own hearts and the hearts of their followers and that they would embrace Islam. They were aware that it took only the reading of a couple of verses, or perhaps a Surah or two, by Muhammad, and listeners were so affected they accepted his message. To them, it seemed like the Qur'an had a magic effect on people.

The elders of the Quraysh were themselves touched by the power of the Qur'an. It was only because they were keenly aware of this profound effect that they resorted to such tactics, warning their people against listening to it and encouraging them to take it frivolously. Indeed, their statement is indicative of how worried they were about the effect of the Qur'an.[19]

    The other pillar of modern Islamist ideology was the Pakistani scholar Sayyid Abul A`la **Mawdudi** (d. 1979). His commentary, *Tafhim al-Qur'an* [Towards Understanding the Qur'an], represents a clarion call for Muslims around the world to establish Shari'a-based Islamic states. His portrayal of Christians was of a divided group, with most blind to the truth of the prophetic message brought by Muhammad. This is seen in the following commentary:

---

[19] Sayyid Qutb, *In the Shade of the Qur'an*, Leicester: The Islamic Foundation, 2002, volume 12, pp329–30.

[Q2:120]: *The Jews and the Christians will never be satisfied with you, O Muhammad, until you follow their way.*

[Mawdudi]: That is, "The reason why these people are displeased with you is not that they are sincere seekers after Truth and that you have failed to make it as clear to them as it should have been. On the contrary, they are offended with you just because you have made the Truth so clear that no loop-hole has been left for them to make religion a paying concern for the gratification of their desires and lusts. Therefore, leave them alone and do not try to reconcile them because it is not possible to please them unless you also adopt the same attitude towards religion as they have adopted. They would have been very happy with you, if you had acted hypocritically like them and made God-worship a cloak for self-worship. It is impossible to please them unless you follow their bad example in your beliefs and practices."[20]

As for the other great school of Islamic thought, Shi'ism, its commentators on the Qur'an tended towards the allegorical over the literal, reflecting the influence of philosophy and Sufism on mainstream Shi'ite thinking. Among the most prominent Shi'ite commentators from early and modern Islam are 'Ali ibn Ibrahim **al-Qummi** (d. 939) and Muhammad **Husayn Tabataba'i** (1903–1982). The latter's twenty volume *al-Mizan fi tafsir al-Qur'an* [Balance in Interpreting the Qur'an] has been translated into many languages and serves as the high point of 20th century Shi'ite exegesis.

In the early 21st century the tension between works of philosophical exegesis, *tafsir bi'l-ra'y*, and the more literalist works of *tafsir bi'l ma'thur* is ever present. Literalist approaches, based on a surface reading of Qur'an and Hadith, are more readily accessible and comprehensible to the Muslim masses, and have been used to justify contemporary radical Islamist policies. In response, modern rationalists, the ideological descendants of the Mu'tazila, insist that the Qur'an should be interpreted according to modern realities rather than contexts from medieval Muslim society. The struggle for the hearts and minds of Muslims is ongoing.

---

[20] http://englishtafsir.com/Quran/2/index.html, accessed 9 August 2017.

Conclusion

What is the relevance of this discussion for Christians in their interactions with Muslims? Several points are pertinent. First, a willingness to engage with not just the Qur'an but also the literature that surrounds it shows a measure of respect for the faith that Muslims hold dear. Respect is a very helpful bridge in building relationships between Christians and Muslims.

Second, a Christian having a facility with Islamic commentaries on the Qur'an is far more likely to receive a hearing from Muslims than is someone who can only refer to Christian or other non-Muslim writing on Islam.

Third, many of the verses of the Qur'an are quite allusive; namely, they require supporting literature in order to be understood. Qur'anic commentaries provide the best means of joining the dots, as it were, when the meaning of a Qur'an verse is not clear.

In the final analysis, Christians who wish to engage with Muslims will need to be speaking in ways that Muslims understand. A knowledge of Islam's sacred text, and the vast body of literature that surrounds it, will greatly help to build the kinds of relationships that allow for discussion of any topic, including difficult questions surrounding the faith of Islam and questions relating to the message of the Gospels.

Bibliography

al-Baydawi, Nasir al-Din Abi Sa'id Abd Allah Abi Umar ibn Muhammad Al-Shirazi. 1996, *Tafsir al-Baydawi al-musamma Anwar al-Tanzil wa Asrar al-Ta'wil*, Beirut: Dar al-Fikr, vol. 2

Berg, H. 2000, *The Development of Exegesis in Early Islam*, Richmond

Boullata, Issa J. (ed.) 2000, *Literary Structures of Religious Meaning in the Qur'an*, London al-Qayrawani, Faris. 1994, *Was Christ Really Crucified?*, Villach, Austria: Light of Life

Gatje, H. 1996, *The Qur'an and its Exegesis*, Oxford: OneWorld

Hamka. 1982, *Tafsir Al-Azhar Juzu'15*, Jakarta: PT Pustaka Panjimas

Ibn Kathir. n.d., *Stories of the Prophets*, trans. R.A. Azami, Riyadh

al-Khazin, A. a. `Ali. n.d., *Lubab al- Ta'wil fi Ma`ani al-Tanzil*, Beirut: Dar al-Thaqafa, n.d., vol. 3

Madelung, W. & Jones, A., (eds), 1987, *The Commentary on the Qur'an by ... al-Tabari*, Oxford

al-Mahalli, Jalal al-Din and al-Suyuti, Jalal al-Din. 2007, *Tafsir al-Jalalayn*, trans. F. Hamza, Amman: Royal Aal al-Bayt Institute for Islamic Thought

McAuliffe, J. D. 1991, *Qur'anic Christians*, Cambridge: Cambridge University Press

McAuliffe, J. D. 2006, *The Cambridge Companion to the Qur'ān*, Cambridge, Cambridge University Press

Newby, Gordon. 1979, "Tafsir Isra'iliyyat." *Journal of the American Academy of Religion*, 47, 685–697

Riddell, P. 1990, *Transferring a Tradition*, Berkeley: Centers for South and Southeast Asian Studies, University of California

Rippin, A. (ed.) 2006, *The Blackwell Companion to the Qur'an*, Malden, Mass.: Blackwell Pub.

Rippin, A. (ed.) 1999, *The Qur'an: Formative Interpretation*, Aldershot: Ashgate

Rippin, A. & Knappert, J. (eds.) 1986, *Textual Sources for the Study of Islam*, Chicago: University of Chicago

Saleh, Walid A. 2004, *The Formation of the Classical Tafsīr Tradition: The Qur'ān Commentary of al-Tha'labī* (d. 427/1035), Leiden: Brill

Sayyid Qutb. 2002, *In the Shade of the Qur'an*, Leicester: The Islamic Foundation

Wensinck, A.J. 1971, *A Handbook of Early Muhammadan Tradition*, Leiden: Brill

Wheeler, Brannon. 2002, *Prophets in the Quran. An Introduction to the Quran and Muslim Exegesis*, London: Continuum,

Zwemer, S. 1905, *The Moslem Doctrine of God*, New York: American Tract Society

THE USE AND ABUSE OF THE QUR'AN IN CHRISTIAN MISSION[1]

Mark Anderson[2]

Integral to much of the controversy over Christian mission to Muslims today are radically different approaches to the Qur'an. In order to heal the growing missiological rift here, we must diligently strive to understand this issue better. Due to the topic's complexity, it has generated much contention and confusion in the church. Hence, if we truly love Christ's Body, we must do our best listening, thinking and disagreeing here, measuring our words not for their rhetorical impact, but rather their clarity and precision. We must if possible think the best of others (1 Cor 13:7). Hence, I begin with the assumption that the five approaches described below have been taken with good intentions. But we must also remember that not since the fall darkened the human mind has "sincerity" been a reliable guide to either goodness or truth. And in all our discussions, we must ensure that our tone reflects the grace we are called to (Col: 4:6). For, properly understood, grace and truth are never in conflict, a point we will return to.

Uses of the Qur'an

Five common uses of the Qur'an are as: 1) a weapon of polemical attack, 2) a bond to "ecumenical" peace, 3) a repository of the "hidden" Gospel, 4) a bridge to biblical truth, and 5) a source to explore and question in dialogue. As I define these uses of the Qur'an, I believe the first three abuse the Qur'an and dishonour Christ and our Muslim friends, while only the fourth and fifth truly

---

[1] This article first appeared in the Evangelical Missiological Society's Occasional Bulletin Spring 2016 issue (vol. 30, no. 2) and is printed here with permission.

[2] Mark Anderson and his wife Cathy served eighteen years in the Middle East interacting with Muslims in a variety of context. Mark has also done extensive studies on Islam, writing his thesis on Jesus' place in the Qur'an. Currently based in Canada, Mark lectures on the Qur'an and Islam both there and abroad. He has recently published *The Qur'an in Context: A Christian Exploration,* IVP Academic, 2016

honour them. In an effort to make my topic more accessible to a broad readership, I begin with my assessments of these five uses of the Qur'an and then explain the criteria that govern my judgments.

1. Using the Qur'an as a Weapon of Polemical Attack

One common use of the Qur'an in Christian mission is as a polemical weapon. Some evangelicals react to the news of Islamist atrocities by turning the Qur'an into an offensive weapon to attack "Islam". This is nothing new. Christians have been doing it for over a millennium. The aim is ostensibly to address Muslim truth claims, which is vital, provided we do it in a Christlike manner. More often than not, however, the real aim is to ridicule and lampoon the Islamic faith, making it appear ignorant or depraved. This may be combined with personal attacks on Muhammad and an overemphasis on the dissimilarity of the Bible and Qur'an.

Those who take this approach may equate the violence of the Qur'an's Medinan *suras*, or chapters, with "true Islam" or employ a radical revisionist critique of the traditional Islamic origins narrative in an attempt to destroy the Muslim faith with one knockout punch. That is, they effectively declare Muslims fools for thinking the traditional origins narrative has any historical basis. Sometimes this involves a blank page approach to Islamic origins, which seeks to remove all confidence in our ever discovering them and render the entire Islamic edifice a sandcastle in the air. The bravado that such lashing out often gives play to confers a false sense of accomplishment, of having "taken ground" in the war of words, and masks an underlying fear. But truth may be used just as easily to harm as heal. The most senseless forms of lashing out involve verbal or physical abuse, even violence, either to Muslims as Muslims or to their sacred symbols. For example, publically burning the Qur'an, as Terry Jones did, or degrading Islam's revered prophet. Whether or not the law of the land protects such behavior, it is sub-Christian and incendiary, as well as ineffective. To use the Muslim scripture to this end abuses it and sows contempt for Muslims, which dishonors Christ.

2. Using the Qur'an as a Bond to "Ecumenical" Peace

The polar opposite of that approach is the "ecumenical" one. Its advocates view the Qur'an as a bond to interfaith unity and aim primarily to promote reconciliation and peaceful relations with Muslims. Since unity and collaboration are their primary concerns, those values inevitably shape the lens through which they view the Muslim scripture. Drawing on such works as Geoffrey Parrinder's *Jesus in the Qur'an* (1995) and Gabriel Said Reynolds's *The Qur'an and its Biblical Subtext* (2008), they strive to maximize the Qur'an's continuity and minimize its discontinuity with the Bible and seek creative ways to "blend" Islam and Christianity. But while the humility to learn from Muslims is always vital, such blended confessions work only by redefining both "Christian" and "Muslim" till some sort of match is found. This approach parallels a larger movement in our society toward interfaith coexistence, a predominant theme in our public discourse.

C. Jonn Block's *The Qur'an in Christian–Muslim Dialogue: Historical and Modern Interpretations* (2014a) offers a recent evangelical example of this. Block believes the Qur'an, instead of attacking orthodox Christianity, champions it against its tritheistic perversion (2014a: 25–26, 39–44). Viewing both the Qur'an and Bible as incomplete revelations, he puts them on an equal footing in the hope that this recognition will impel Christians and Muslims alike to pursue "the humble orthodoxy that allows mutuality in spite of apparent contradiction" and accept their respective scriptures' ambiguity as a "divinely intended quality of revelation" (Block 2014b: 16, 19). Hence, Block hears the Qur'an as an "ecumenical voice" that allowed for the salvation of Christians, while striving to correct their theological excesses (2014b: 17). He writes that "Muhammad was very possibly the seal of the prophets of Yahweh, just as Jesus is indeed a servant of Allah." It is on this basis that he speaks of our "mutually agreed upon transcendent and omnipotent One True God" and of the virtual indistinguishability of Islam from Christianity and vice-versa (2014b: 19, 20).

By giving the Qur'an an ecumenical narrative, ecumenists render it an ecumenical scripture, interpreted very differently from how it is interpreted by traditional Islam. They effectively Christianise the Qur'an and so subvert it in the name of peace by refusing to take it seriously on its own terms. Having done so, they must then explain the disjunction between their conception of proto-Islam and Islam's classical manifestations. Though Block goes to some length to provide a historical rationale for his reading of the Qur'an, he fails to offer a satisfactory basis for his hypothesis. One example of this is seen in his presentation of Isho'yahb III of Adiabene, an early Christian source on Islam. Block attributes to historian Robert G. Hoyland the view that Isho'yahb never considered Islam "as a 'separate phenomenon' from Christianity" (Block 2014: 154). But taken in its original context, the statement Block cites (Hoyland 1997: 179) does not mean what he says it does. Hoyland "did not at all intend to say that Isho'yahb did not distinguish the Muslims ... from the Christians" (Hoyland 2015, pers. comm., 12 July). Block appears to mistake for an acceptance of the divine origin of the Arabs' religion the early Christian recognition that God had sent the Arabs to punish them for their sins. To do so he must disregard the preponderance of early Christian evidence on Islam, which points to a great gulf between the two faiths. What Hoyland says of Fred M. Donner's ecumenical approach is equally relevant here: though it is a worthy aim harmoniously to combine Muslims in Islam's early period with their fellow monotheists, "it is concerned more with our modern world than with that of Muhammad and his followers" (Hoyland 2012: 576).

A popular version of the ecumenical approach comes in the common claim that the Qur'an's message is essentially that of the Bible, which usually boils down to something like: "Since we both believe in God and Jesus, our specific beliefs beyond that need not divide us. We just need to love each other and live out whatever truths we have each been given. What matters supremely is that we get along together." Proponents of this are right to stress the urgency of peaceful coexistence, but not to the extent that they sideline vital doctrinal truths. They also take the Meccan *suras*' nonviolent approach as representative of "true Islam," either ignore or creatively reinterpret the Qur'an's violent content and join our government leaders in making Muslim violence seem somehow un-Islamic. This involves disregarding most of what the earliest sources tell us about Muhammad and the Muslim conquest in order to make him and his scripture fit the frame they have made for them.

For obvious reasons, this approach has broad appeal—indeed, who would not wish its take on Islam were true? But no credible historian takes its nonviolent Muhammad to be complete. And any presentation of the Qur'an that limits itself to either of its approaches to power is inadequate since neither "half" of the Qur'an can fairly represent the whole. Yet so effective have the purveyors of this approach been that many people have no idea the Qur'an's other "half" even exists and understandably many evangelicals have been swept along by this tide. Though peacemaking is clearly commanded by scripture (Rom 12:18), we are called not just to love Muslims, but to love them as Jesus loved—with both grace *and* truth (John 1:17; 20:21). And while the two scriptures share many beliefs about God, they disagree strongly on his character.

3.   A Repository of the "Hidden" Gospel

Some evangelicals marshal qur'anic texts in such a way as to demonstrate that, if only you know where to find it, the Qur'an's "real meaning" is the message of the gospel, narrowly defined. These good folk are evangelists, but their use of the Qur'an is similar to that of ecumenists since they too attempt to make the Qur'an agree with the Bible at points where the two scriptures are actually very much at odds. But since their goal is conversion of some kind, they focus not just on qur'anic teaching concerning God's unity, but also on faith in Jesus as the only source of saving grace. They may also lower the bar for potential converts by either omitting the Trinity or talking it away since they deem it unnecessary to salvation and more trouble than it is worth.

One example of this is the pseudonymously written *The Belief of Isma'il*, which seeks to prove from the Qur'an that "*it is only by the Grace and Mercy of Allah in Isa al-Masih (pbuh) that we can be accepted by Allah*" (2006: 77, author's emphasis). But the Qur'an gives no indication whatsoever that Jesus did anything for the "redemption of the world," a category entirely foreign to it. It also states repeatedly that, besides the mercy of God's sovereign choice, he forgives sins on the basis of repentance, faith and pious deeds (Q2:277; 3:195; 5:94; 24:47–56; 29:7; 33:35; 46:31). Thus, the Qur'an uses words like "expiation" *(kaffara)* always with reference to the believer's acts of piety and charity (Q5:45, 89, 95). As Q11:114 says, "Good deeds remove evil deeds". Ultimately, only the believer whose good deeds outweigh her bad earns God's pardon (Q7:8–9; 21:47; 23:102–103; 101:6–9, cf. 3:30; 18:49; 54:52–53). But Ibn Isma'il does not allow the Qur'an to speak for itself and limits beliefs "essential to salvation" to those biblical truths he can make relatively uncontroversial to Muslims.

This use of the Qur'an always implicitly grants it authority equal to that of the Bible, although some—including Ibn Isma'il—make the point explicit by asserting that "*This is what Allah said to the prophet Muhammad (pbuh)" (2006: 20, author's emphasis). Only by seriously distorting the Qur'an's meaning can Ibn Isma'il hold to historic Christian creeds and profess faith in the Qur'an. It is one thing to observe partially shared beliefs and allow such common ground to lead to further dialogue, but quite another to assert that Muslims ought to believe anything *because* the Qur'an tells them to. Though we can rejoice over every point the Qur'an agrees with the Bible on—just as we rejoice to see our own culture echo biblical truths—such agreement categorically does not make the Qur'an "God's Word" to Muhammad. According to Ibn Isma'il, by following Muhammad and obeying the Qur'an, *truly understood*, we follow Jesus since Muhammad followed Jesus and was a true prophet of God. As with the "ecumenists," Ibn Isma'il can only draw such conclusions by rewriting the Islamic origins narrative such that the Qur'an says what he wants it to say.

4. A Bridge to Biblical Truth

It is possible, however, to "bridge" from the Qur'an to the Bible without compromising biblical truth. One such approach is that of Kevin Greeson, who describes the "Camel method" Muslim-background believers taught him as a "bridge from error to truth" (2014). Essentially, it involves the evangelist's using the Qur'an's "flickers of truth" as talking points to guide his hearer to the Bible. Though some of what Greeson does with the qur'anic text goes beyond its original intent, he uses one of the Qur'an's most positive passages on Jesus, Q3:42–55, to establish that he is holy, all-powerful and knows the way to heaven. Greeson connects Jesus' virgin birth to his sinlessness and highlights his ability to raise the dead, both points making him unique among God's prophets. Drawing all this together with the passage's teaching that God took Jesus to be with him in heaven (Q3:55), Greeson concludes that Jesus knows the way to heaven because "He Himself has traveled the straight path from Allah to earth and returned to Allah in heaven." He then asks, Who would be the best guide to heaven, someone who has gone there himself or not? Hearers who conclude that Jesus must be our best guide are then open to looking at what the Bible says and leaving the Qur'an behind (2014). Greeson is emphatic that he simply uses the Qur'an to facilitate the transition to the biblical text (2010).

Greeson claims his method enables the Muslim to see "from the text of his own Qur'an ... that Isa is far more than a prophet," but he acknowledges that not every Muslim will see that. Although he goes too far when he says that the Qur'an teaches Jesus' "divine attributes" (2014), it is certainly understandable why qur'anic doublespeak on Jesus—its simultaneous honouring and marginalization of him—might send readers in that direction. Taking Q3:42–55 apart from the Qur'an's larger context, the passage does appear—especially to Christian readers—to point to Jesus' deity. It does not actually do that, although it should not surprise us that Muslim background believers may see the Qur'an in that way and find it effective in evangelizing their friends. Essentially, Greeson's method just uses the Qur'an's own ambiguity to crack the door, as it were, and let all who long for more truth to discover what awaits them in the light outside.

Greeson's use of Muslim language enables the listener to move from the familiar to the unfamiliar. Although he begins with the Qur'an, he says he invests the Qur'an with no more authority than Paul's use of pagan poetry did (Acts 17:28). Rather, he uses the qur'anic text simply to connect with the listener, prompt him to question his faith, gauge his hunger for God and guide him to truth. Greeson also couples his use of the Qur'an with leading questions, enabling the Muslim to "gently draw a contrast ... between Isa and another prophet whom he knows all too well" without ever mentioning the latter's name (2014). Thus, Greeson graciously points hearers to the biblical way to God.

5. A Source to Explore and Question

A fifth use of the Qur'an takes it seriously, treats it with respect, interprets it in context and graciously contrasts it with the Bible. Two examples of this approach immediately come to mind, the first being the Anglican-sponsored "Building Bridges Seminar." Since 2002 the seminar has produced a steady stream of publications with an emphasis on qur'anic and biblical studies pursued in a context of open enquiry, respect and friendship. The other is David W. Shenk's collaboration with Badru D. Kateregga in *A Muslim and a Christian in Dialogue* (1999).

Two other examples are A.H. Mathias Zahniser's *The Mission and Death of Jesus in Islam and Christianity* (2008) and Gordon Nickel's *The Gentle Answer to the Muslim Accusation of Biblical Falsification* (2014). Zahniser carefully studies the totality of qur'anic teaching on the end of Jesus' mission and death in order to build a case for a different interpretation of the so-called "crucifixion verse" (Q4:157) from the one believed by most Muslims. By Zahniser's interpretation, Jesus did not escape crucifixion, but rather endured it, as most early Muslim commentators attest. Most Muslims also hold to the notion either that the biblical text has been corrupted or falsified beyond usefulness or else that we no longer have the Gospel God allegedly gave to Jesus. In whichever version, this theory seemingly resolves the huge discrepancy between the qur'anic presentation of the Christian scripture and a New Testament that bears almost no resemblance to it. It also enables Muslims "to rebuff any arguments based by Christians on the Bible" (Watt 1991: 30), which is why Muslims have made the falsification theory so central to their polemic (Goldziher, cited in Nickel 2011: 2). The best way to counter this accusation is by gently and patiently examining the qur'anic texts Muslims use to support it and demonstrating its fatal flaws, which is precisely what Nickel does.

As encouraging as all these studies are, much remains to be done in terms of respectfully exploring the Qur'an. A contrastive study will also enable us to explore the qur'anic approach to coercion and reply to Shabbir Akhtar's assertion that Jesus was "allergic to worldly power" (Akhtar 1991: 27). Among other things, we must effectively question the Qur'an's claim of monotheistic purity, its implicit claim to honour Christ and its claim to be the Bible's sequel.

However, addressing issues Muslims and Christians are deeply divided over calls for wisdom and grace. One tool to help facilitate dialogue is the ABC approach advocated by *Crucial Conversations: Tools for talking when stakes are high* (Patterson *et al* 2012: 170–172). The ABC stands for *agree*, *build* and *contrast*. Unfortunately, the higher the stakes, the keener we often are to disagree. Finding something genuinely to *agree* on right out of the gate minimizes argument, helping to legitimize your partner's concerns and allay her fear that you care most about being right. Once you have established common ground and your partner feels heard, you can *build* by seeking a broader understanding of the topic. That then enables you to *contrast* the two positions and explore differences and concerns constructively. But instead of disagreeing, contrasting involves laying your respective views out side-by-side and discussing them from a position of mutual respect.

By enabling both partners to maintain their integrity, this approach can transform competition into collaboration and allow both to ask good questions—even hard ones.

Criteria for Judging Our Uses of the Qur'an

How do I defend my assessment of these uses of the Qur'an? On the basis of four criteria, which I believe are also the factors driving Christians to make such different uses of the Qur'an in the first place. Those criteria are: 1) our approach to the study of world religions, 2) our choice of the Qur'an's narrative, 3) our grasp of its worldview and 4) our understanding of our primary calling in mission. These factors both shape and judge our use of the Qur'an—whether or not it honours Christ.

1. Our Approach to the Study of World Religions

Our study of world religions always comes with two great temptations: either crediting the other religion or its scripture with more truth than is really there or, conversely, refusing to acknowledge truths it actually evidences. Since both tendencies distort reality, both are mistaken. Anyone tempted to equate the Qur'an with the Bible needs to recognize that syncretism poses an ever-present danger and that no marginalization of Jesus is ever biblically acceptable (John 14:16, Acts 4:12, Phil 2:9–11). On the other hand, all truth truly is God's truth; even a total lie is just truth twisted out of shape. Yet even if Houston is 97 degrees accurate in plotting the course of a space flight, the spaceship is still going to miss its goal. Simply affirming that the Qur'an contains some light is not to say its light is strong enough to guide us to salvation. So we must not allow fear—whether of syncretism or of being unfairly labelled syncretistic—to keep us from speaking the truth about the Qur'an (2 Tim 1:7).

2. Our Choice of the Qur'an's Narrative

Due to its complexity, the issue of narrative requires more concentrated attention than any of the other criteria. And as we saw with uses two and three above, this issue is of critical importance because changing the narrative gives us the power to change the Qur'an's meaning. Angelika Neuwirth argues that the Qur'an is the "transcript of an orally performed, open-ended" prophetic monologue rather than a "written, premeditated corpus of prophetical sayings" (Neuwirth, 2009). Its every word is centred in Muhammad's struggle for "God's cause" in his native Arabia. On hermeneutical grounds, Neuwirth says we must read it as a series of texts growing out of "lively scenes from the emergence of a community" under Muhammad (Neuwirth 2003: 6). Examples of her point abound. For example, Q8:67–69 addresses the problem of the early Muslims' love of booty and Q8:70–71 speaks of the prophet's having enslaved captives taken in battle. Hence, Muhammad and the Muslim community, or *umma*, engaged in military conquest and considered booty and slavery to be divinely regulated. In that sense, the Qur'an represents an immense cache of historical data.

Despite the centrality of Muhammad's story to its recitations, however, they include only faint glimmers of it. The Qur'an pays considerable attention to narratives from the past, but is quite averse to supplying contemporary narrative. Muhammad's recitations came in the midst of some very stormy events, but instead of recounting those events, the Qur'an "merely refers to them; and in doing so, it has a tendency not to name names" (Cook 1983: 69). The qur'anic author often speaks as "I" or "we" or alternates between the two (e.g. Q90:1–4) and addresses "you" in singular and plural (e.g. Q94:1–4). But usually no one is identified, leaving us to piece the story together from the mention of an unnamed town and other fragmentary details. He speaks of Christians (*nasara*) and the "sacred precinct" (e.g. Q5:1). But what kind of Christians and which "sacred precinct"? These and a host of other questions find their answer only in the Qur'an's narrative context. However, being well-known to those who first heard the recitations, all such background information was left unstated, making the Qur'an singularly unhelpful to us as a historical source, taken on its own. Hence, the reader must bring to the qur'anic text some knowledge of Muhammad's prophetic career and historical context.

But this is where things get really complex because our earliest narrative of Islamic origins is quite late—i.e. nearly two centuries after the fact—and greatly embellished and distorted by piety and polemics, among other things. The biography of Muhammad, or *sira*, relies primarily on the Hadith, or reports about Muhammad and his companions. But while some of the Hadith seem accurate, many are contradictory: either inaccurate or totally contrived. This is like having your star witness in court seriously exaggerate one third of the time and straight-out lie another third. Do you angrily order him off the stand, even though you know some of what he says is vital to the court's reaching a just verdict? Or do you painstakingly sift through his testimony to see what of it is corroborated by other evidence and thus locate the part that is actually reliable? Granted, trashing the Muslim tradition is the far easier route to take. But as we will see, it leads us nowhere. The Hadith are highly problematic, but how we handle them decides our approach to the traditional Islamic origins narrative they give rise to, which in turn shapes our hermeneutic (Madigan 1995: 351) and our consequent use of the Qur'an.

Poor Solutions to the Narrative Problem

Historically Western scholars and missionaries alike have interpreted the Qur'an with the traditional Islamic origins narrative in mind. Although they rejected miraculous and blatantly polemical elements, beyond that they were largely uncritical, thus making the traditional origins narrative appear solidly founded.

For more than a millennium that worked well enough, but in the late nineteenth century Western scholars began taking more sceptical approaches as qur'anic studies started catching up to biblical criticism. The revisionism this produced was very mixed in its results, its various proponents motivated by either polemics, ecumenism or secular rationalism. The best-known polemicist claims the Qur'an originated as a Syro-Aramiac Christian lectionary (Luxenberg 2009). Others argue that we know almost nothing about the origins of Islam. Some have even questioned Muhammad's existence, although no credible scholars currently do. Ecumenically-minded scholars view the Bible and Qur'an as complementary, the latter allegedly attacking only a heretical, tritheistic version of Christianity, which they say was present in Muhammad's Arabia. They thus transform the Muslim prophet into a champion of Christian orthodoxy and discover an underlying unity between Christianity and Islam. Secular scholars usually work with a linear model of religious development, hypothesizing that the Qur'an itself is the product of a lengthy evolutionary process that occurred in the largely monotheistic Fertile Crescent, not in pagan Arabia. To allow for this, they reject the traditional sources as being so polluted that the origins narrative they gave rise to tells us nothing of the true origins of Islam, but only what later generations wanted to believe about them. One scholar bolsters the position that Islam actually emerged in a monotheistic environment by postulating that the Qur'an uses "idolatry" only figuratively to attack not polytheism—as the Hadith maintain—but rather retrograde monotheism (Hawting 1999). By the 1980s a sharp division had developed between the radical revisionists and those unprepared altogether to jettison the traditional origins narrative, with each side vehemently accusing the other of ignoring the obvious.

Everyone agrees on the Hadith's historical unreliability, the immediate cause of the division. At issue is only the extent of their unreliability and how to respond. The problem is that, by rejecting the Hadith either entirely or substantially, the revisionists made the Qur'an's milieu an open question. So widely varied are the scholarly answers given to it that Patricia Crone likens the situation to one where we encounter Jesus' quotations from the Hebrew Bible in the Gospels but are unsure if he was Jewish or whether his quotations were imported from outside his tradition. In addition, suppose the Gospels' geographical markers were so few and so vague that scholars disputed whether Jesus lived in Mesopotamia, Palestine or Greece. Such a degree of uncertainty would render the Gospels' meaning exceedingly elusive, which is precisely the situation we face in qur'anic studies (Crone 2009).

Revisionism's more basic problem is that, despite its criticism of tradition, it is remarkably uncritical of its own underlying rationalistic hostility to tradition. Inherent in the Historical Method is the premise that tradition does not mediate history, making the historian duty-bound "if possible, to see through tradition to the history that might (or indeed might not) exist behind it" (Provan, Long & Longman 2003: 24). Most evangelical revisionists stress how much wider the time gap is between Muhammad and the traditional sources on him, compared to Jesus and the New Testament documents. Their point is valid, but they fail to mention that a much larger gap exists between the earliest Old Testament documents and most of the events they describe. So if we reject the Muslim tradition's authenticity on that ground, we must also reject most Old Testament history—of, say, the patriarchs and the Exodus. Rather than taking so uncritical an approach, we need to remain open to testimony of all kinds, including that of tradition.

A Sound Solution

Though entirely consistent with his view of revelation, the qur'anic author's utter lack of concern about framing his content with intelligible context is highly problematic for qur'anic interpreters, as is the matter of hadith authenticity. The encouraging news, however, is that while fine scholars still position themselves on both sides of the Islamic origins divide, a consensus now seems gradually to be forming, as historians sift through Late Antique evidence with Islamic origins in mind. There is sufficient early non-Muslim evidence for us to accept that an Arabian trader named Muhammad presented himself as a prophet in the early seventh century, calling his people to abandon their polytheism and embrace his version of monotheism. Upon moving to Yathrib, he assumed theocratic rule and led his followers to conquer in God's name. There is no sound reason for us to question this much of the traditional origins narrative. Most scholars also accept the evidence from a large cache of ancient Qur'an manuscripts discovered in Sana'a in the early 1970s as establishing the fact that the written Qur'an text was undergoing editing during the late seventh and early eighth centuries, which also accords with Muslim tradition (Small 2013). Other manuscript evidence points to an even earlier date. Furthermore, there is a growing body of evidence for the general authenticity of early Arabic poetry, which Islamic scholarship deemed an invaluable guide to the Qur'an's overall context (Bauer 2010).

We might term this approach "critical realism" because we are as *open to* as we are *critical of* the traditional sources. This stems from a realistic appreciation of the challenges inherent in reconstructing history—especially ancient history—where certainty refers simply to the integrity of our evidence and reasoning since demanding absolute proof here is fruitless. Whether we like it or not, we all come to the Qur'an with some kind of hypothetical narrative in mind. But critical realists refuse dogmatic revisionists' damning of all the Hadith simply due to either their oral and relatively late origins or their Muslim bias—as if other sources are not biased. Instead, we scrutinize all the available data to determine which elements in the traditional narrative are confirmed or contradicted by early independent sources. We also refuse to pronounce on what did not exist based on missing evidence. We thus base our verdict on the preponderance of the historical evidence, recognizing that we have much to lose by embracing radical revisionism, despite the apparent freedom it offers.

But while the early non-Muslim sources afford us ample support for the traditional biography of Muhammad in broad outline, we remain sceptical about many of its details—such things as its account of Jewish treachery and its idealized view of Muhammad, Mecca and the early *umma*. Recent studies have also shown that an astonishingly high 52% of the qur'anic text consists of repeated, oral-formulaic material, suggesting "that Muhammad (or Allah or the archangel Gabriel) was seemingly well-versed in the techniques of folklorist oral transmission" (Bannister 2014: 274: 57). Synthesizing all of the available evidence, we thus conclude that Muhammad was an early seventh-century trader turned prophet, operating in a polytheistic Hijazi milieu and that "Islam began as an avowed reformation of previous monotheism and pagan polytheism" (Graham 1983: 66). Hence, we find no major disjunction between Islam as it developed under Muhammad and classical Islam.

3. Our Grasp of the Qur'an's Worldview

Besides the question of milieu, there is another aspect of context we must reckon with to grasp the Qur'an's meaning accurately. A scripture's theology is not a catalogue of disparate ideas. Rather, each of its teachings interacts with and gives shape to the others within its conceptual framework. Hence, we must understand what the components of the qur'anic worldview are and how they interrelate. For example: How does the Qur'an view God, humankind and the relationship between them? What is sin, how does it affect that relationship and how do we obtain salvation? What role do prophets and revelation play in that and what is the nature of scripture? What place does the community of faith hold, what is its mission in the world and how does it fulfil that mission? How does the Qur'an view spirituality in all its dimensions? And how do all these things compare to their biblical counterparts?

Using such a comparative approach to the qur'anic worldview is like pointing out similarities and differences of colour, line and shading between two great paintings. It enables us to appreciate the Qur'an's relation to the biblical thought world better: both its distinctiveness from and its continuity with biblical theology. This is vital because the Qur'an often suggests more agreement with the Bible than actually exists. Despite obvious similarities, the two worldviews embody "quite different outlines, characters and structures" (Adams 1984: 306, 287). And when doctrines seem more similar than they in fact are, such similarity obstructs understanding. Numerous findings from such a study of its worldview reflect the Qur'an's having originated in a polytheistic, tribal milieu and Muhammad's desire to establish a new religio-political entity like the Christian, Jewish and Mazdean (Zoroastrian) states and empires in the surrounding lands. Only against this backdrop can we gain a true appreciation of the qur'anic approach to Jesus.

On the basis of this combined historical and worldview, external and internal, evidence, we can conclude that the Qur'an was given to provide two things, namely the community's *raison d'etre* and its ultimate authority. To these two, the *umma* has very understandably added a third: most Muslims view the Qur'an as their only means of direct access to God. For they believe they encounter God existentially not through qur'anic teachings per se, but rather through the Qur'an's linguistic being—its presence in their lives as the eternal word of God—primarily by means of recitation and calligraphy. And in all three respects, the Qur'an presents a direct challenge to us as Christians. First, it displaces the church, which Christ loved and died for, with the Muslim *umma* as the people of God. And since an element of coercion has been central to the Muslim community's mission from almost the start, this represents an implicit denial of Jesus' approach to loving our enemies and freedom of belief. Second, the Muslim scripture constitutes itself, its prophet and implicitly the tradition that comes from them as the final authority for faith and practice. And third, because Muslims view the Qur'an as the only physical manifestation of the divine, it stands functionally in the place of Jesus as the way to God. Since the Qur'an challenges biblical faith and teaching on so many levels, it is natural that our response should be commensurate with its challenge.

4. Our Primary Calling in Mission

The final criterion for judging the various uses of the Qur'an lies in what we view as our primary calling in Christian mission, whether we relate to Muslims first and foremost as apologists, peacemakers, evangelists or friends. Our different answers here derive from how we view the challenge facing us in the world, the nature and scope of God's solution and our place in that solution. It should be evident by now that I view both polemics and seeking "ecumenical" unity with Muslims as unbiblical. However, we should not discount their biblical counterparts, apologetics/elenctics and peacemaking/service, which, together with evangelism/church planting, comprise our missional task.

The key thing is that we follow Jesus' example in all three. Scripture clearly shows him combatting error with truth and unmasking evil (John 15:22; Matt 5–7). But if we take that as our supreme calling in relation to Muslims, we tend to make things black-and-white and overlook the many ways truth can appear in other religions. For clarity's sake, we make categorical pronouncements without sufficiently seasoning our words with grace (Col 4:6). Jesus, by contrast, was quite content to leave people uncertain about some things in order to ensure that God's heart for sinners was unmistakably clear to them (Luke 4:22). Many Christians fear that following Jesus here would be reckless, but how can we truly call him Lord and "improve on" his way?

Scripture also extolls peacemaking and doing good to others (Ps 133, Rom 12:18, Gal 6:10). But if we view that as our primary calling, we tend to restrict ourselves to those points we agree with Muslims on and downplay our deeper differences. Yet anyone reading the Gospels can see that Jesus did not make peace with everyone. In fact, he sometimes seemed intent on making enemies. Not that he really was so disposed, but he absolutely did not mince words when his handlers—if he had had such—would surely have told him to tone it down. Jesus' approach may seem ludicrous today, a quick way to earn a bad reputation. But he clearly did not care about that, prompting us to ask whether we value our good name over true peace.

Scripture likewise commands us to make disciples everywhere (Matt 28:18–20). But if we consider that our primary calling, we tend to care less about what means we use so long as we make disciples. We may reduce the standard of discipleship to make recruitment easier. But Jesus was very careful about the means he used to attract followers and often seemed determined to weed out as many as possible. Some may wonder how we can be expected to follow him there if we aim to plant churches. But it is ultimately his job to build his church and we gain nothing by building carelessly, which he clearly did not do (Matt 16:18, 1 Cor 3:10–12).

What grounds and centres our apologetic, peacemaking and evangelistic tasks is viewing them as aspects of a higher calling to extend true friendship to Muslims. This is our supreme missional calling. For in absolutely everything Jesus did, he was our friend. That included walking with us down dusty roads, bearing our burdens and loving us at all times (Prov 17:17; 18:24, Luke 10:25–37). It involved telling us the truth with scalpel-like precision when we were convinced we did not need it (Prov 27:5–6). It included loving us to the end and even dying for us when we shunned and crucified him (John 13:1; 15:13). Fulfilling our commission involves being the kind of friends to others that Jesus was to us (John 20:21, 1 Pet 2:21). Doing so will shine light into the darkness of some Muslims, enable us to be reconciled and do good to some and lead some to follow God's glorious Son and join his church. But as we cannot control anyone's response to our message, so also we are not answerable for their response. Offering true friendship is responsibility enough for us.

Biblically, apologetics/elenctics, peacemaking/service and evangelism/church planting are all important. But considering any of them our supreme calling opens us to the danger of that "results" orientation so prevalent in our culture, which emphasizes quantitative outcomes to the extent that the end justifies the means. Without a firm grounding in the moral character of God, our apologetic, peacemaking or evangelistic concerns very easily decide everything else. Thus, we turn the Qur'an into a weapon of attack, a bond of peace or a repository of hidden truth, when it is actually none of the above. Viewing our three missional tasks as aspects of our higher calling to extend true friendship to Muslims helps us avoid such excess.

Grace and Truth's Hour is Now, Always

Bearing witness to truth is no less central to our mission than it was to Jesus' mission (John 18:37, Acts 1:8). We must "all of us speak the truth to our neighbours," but how we do that is just as important as what we say: if we do not speak humbly, we are unfaithful to the truth (Eph 4:25, Jas 3:14–16). Despite the knee-jerk appeal of either fight or flight, neither is worthy of Christ. We must not attack Muslims with their Qur'an or abuse it by denying that it issues a challenge to Christianity, which is a form of flight. Positively, we simply tell the good news of Jesus. But negatively, since most Muslims believe they have an ironclad case, we must gently and patiently offer them clarity by demonstrating the profound uncertainty of their truth claims.

From childhood onward Muslims are taught that friendship with God is utterly impossible. Yet that is the very thing we invite them to. We cannot angrily scream our invitation, muddle it together with some lesser appeal or mutter it under our breath. Friends alone speak convincingly of friendship. We must not let our "grace" get in the way of truth or our "truth telling" justify ungraciousness. But this union of seeming opposites does not come easily. Only led by the same Spirit that led Jesus can we find grace and truth's authentic oneness, yielding the same gracious witness and vulnerable boldness that he and his apostles modelled. By the Spirit, we are also strengthened to believe that Jesus unleashed a power in the world unlike anything before or since—Islamism included. It is ours just to align ourselves with his unstoppable power and leave the results with him for both the healing of his Church and the salvation of the world.

Selected Bibliography

Adams, Charles J. 1984. Islam and Christianity: The Opposition of Similarities. In Savory, Roger H. & Agius, Dionisius A. (eds.). *Logos Islamikos: Studia Islamica in Honorem Georgii Michaelis Wickens*. Toronto: Pontifical Institute of Mediaeval Studies.

Akhtar, Shabbir 1991. *Final Imperative: An Islamic Theology of Liberation*. London: Bellew Publishing Co.

Bannister, Andrew G. 2014. *An Oral-Formulaic Study of the Qur'an*. Lanham: Lexington Books.

Block, C. Jonn 2014a. *The Qur'an in Christian–Muslim Dialogue: Historical and Modern Interpretations*. New York: Routledge.

---------- 2014b. "Competing Christian Narratives on the Qur'an." Bridging the Divide Collaboration. Accessed May 1, 2015. http://btdnetwork.org/wp-content/uploads/2014/08/Competing-Christian-narratives-on-the-Quran-C-Jonn-Block.pdf

A Common Word Document 2007. Amman, Jordan: The Royal Aal al-Bayt Institute for Islamic Thought. Viewed May 18, 2015. www.acommonword.com/the-acw-document

Cook, Michael 1983. *Muhammad*. Oxford: Oxford University Press.

Crone, Patricia 2009. Opening remarks in Angelika Neuwirth. The 'Late Antique Qur'an': Jewish—Christian Liturgy, Hellenic Rhetoric and Arabic Language. Lecture at the Institute for Advanced Studies, Princeton, June 3. Viewed October 12, 2013.
http://www.yovisto.com/video/11805

Graham, William 1983. Islam in the Mirror of Ritual. In *Islam's Understanding of Itself*, Hovannisian, Richard G. & Vryonis, Speros Jr. (eds.). Malibu: Undena Publications.

Greeson, Kevin 2010. Interview: Kevin Greeson of the Camel Method. *Biblical Missiology* [e-journal]. Viewed May 7, 2015.
http://biblicalmissiology.org/2010/04/21/interview-kevin-greeson-of-camel-method/

---------- 2014. *The Camel: How Muslims Are Coming to Faith in Christ!* Revised (Kindle).

Hawting, G.R. 1999. *The Idea of Idolatry and the Emergence of Islam: From Polemic to History*. New York: Cambridge University Press.

Hoyland, Robert G. 2012. Muhammad and the Believers: At the Origins of Islam by Fred M. Donner reviewed in *International Journal of Middle East Studies*, 44 (3) p576.

Ibn Isma'il, Adan 2006. *The Belief of Isma'il*. Minneapolis: Isma'il Books.

Kateregga, Badru D. & Shenk, David W. 1981. *A Muslim and a Christian in Dialogue*. Grand Rapids: William B. Eerdmans Publishing.

Luxenberg, Christoph 2007. *The Syro–Aramaic Reading of the Koran: A Contribution to the Decoding of the Language of the Koran.* Berlin: Verlag Hans Schiler.

Madigan, Daniel 1995. "Reflections on Some Current Directions in Qur'anic Studies." *Muslim World* vol. 85: 351.

Neuwirth, Angelika 2003. "Qur'an and History–A Disputed Relationship: Some Reflections on Qur'anic History and History in the Qur'an." *Journal of Qur'anic Studies* vol. 5: 6.

------------2009. The 'Late Antique Qur'an': Jewish–Christian Liturgy, Hellenic Rhetoric and Arabic Language. Lecture at the Institute for Advanced Studies, Princeton, June 3. Viewed October 12, 2013.
http://www.yovisto.com/video/11805

Nickel, Gordon D. 2011. *Narratives of Tampering in the Earliest Commentaries on the Qur'an.* Leiden: Brill.

------------ 2014. *The Gentle Answer to the Muslim Accusation of Biblical Falsification* Calgary: Bruton Gate.

Parrinder, Geoffrey 1995. *Jesus in the Qur'an.* Oxford: Oneworld.

Patterson, K. Grenny, J. McMillan, R. and Switzler A. 2012. *Crucial Conversations: Tools for Talking When Stakes Are High*, 2nd ed. New York: McGraw-Hill.

Provan I, Long P & Longman T, III 2003. *A Biblical History of Israel.* Louisville: Westminster John Knox Press.

Reynolds, Gabriel Said 2008. *The Qur'an and its Biblical Subtext.* London: Routledge.

Small, Keith E. 2011. *Textual Criticism and Qur'an Manuscripts.* Lanham: Lexington Books.

---------- 2013. "Qur'an Manuscripts: Thoughts on How the Text Was Preserved and Passed On." Lecture, Al-Maktoum

College of Higher Education, Dundee, Scotland, February 20. Viewed November 5, 2014
https://www.youtube.com/watch?v=Hou4JcHo67o

Zahniser, A. H. Mathias 2008. *The Mission and Death of Jesus in Islam and Christianity*. Maryknoll: Orbis Book

www.ingramcontent.com/pod-product-compliance
Lightning Source LLC
Chambersburg PA
CBHW072055290426
44110CB00014B/1687